Forces Sweethearts

Forces Sweethearts

JOANNA LUMLEY

Foreword by **JILLY COOPER**

BLOOMSBURY

First published in Great Britain 1993
Bloomsbury Publishing Limited, 2 Soho Square, London W1V 5DE

Text copyright © 1993 by Joanna Lumley
Foreword copyright © 1993 by Jilly Cooper

The moral right of the authors has been asserted

A CIP catalogue record for this book
is available from the British Library

ISBN 0 7475 1339 2

Designed by Fielding Rowinski
Typeset by Florencetype Limited, Kewstoke, Avon
Printed in Great Britain by Bath Press Colourbooks, Glasgow

For my mother and father

A silver powder compact bought by Captain James Rutherford Lumley in the Street Called Straight in Damascus in 1942. The silversmith imprinted 'Beatrice', written in my father's hand, on the lid. Tiny scenes of Syria appear round the rim: camels, palm trees and Arabian dhows in full sail. He gave it to my mother in Abbottabad when he returned to India a year later, in August 1943. From there he was posted to Burma with the 3/6th Gurkhas in the Second Chindit Campaign.

CONTENTS

FOREWORD

I first met Joanna Lumley in 1970 at a time of great conflict. She was starring as one of four debs in a comedy series I had written for the BBC. The screaming matches on the set were pyrotechnic. An Australian director had tried to take the whole thing down-market. All those involved, including the actors, kept changing the scripts and threatened to take their names off the series when these changes weren't accepted. Heavy reproof descended constantly from on high because of the blueness of the jokes. People stalked out, everyone fought – except Joanna.

She was not only wonderfully beautiful in the part – even looking stunning in a bath-cap with no hair showing – but also utterly professional. She knew her lines, was always on time and always brought something extra and original to the character she was playing. More important, she was sweet to everyone, a still centre, who listened to all of us – but never backbiting or taking sides – and put in a wonderful performance, which I like to think put her several rungs up the ladder to stardom.

So it is fitting that she has once again provided a still centre, in the bittersweet subject of love in times of war. This book is a beautiful anthology full of prose, poetry and pictures that bring a lump to the throat as well as warming the heart.

During war people fall in love at lightning speed and express their feelings with spontaneity and passion, because there may be no tomorrow. Loss is also more poignant: one thinks of the desperately painful knowledge that a sweetheart has been killed in action, while his tender love letters keep on arriving through the post, or of the agonising discovery by a soldier husband far from home that his wife is being unfaithful.

But there are plenty of happier notes in this anthology: brides' dresses made of parachute silk; a major's enchanting letter to a two-year-old daughter he has never seen; and, above all, the constant dreams of peacetime:

Oh yes, Dorfie girl, won't it be topping to sit on a cool shady bank and watch the trout . . .

Only this morning, Relate sadly reported a fifty per cent breakdown in marriages. It is therefore inspiring to find in this anthology how many couples endured separation, deprivation and great poverty in the early stages of marriage, but are still happily together celebrating their golden weddings. Here is an unselfishness, a stoicism, a regard for the intense preciousness of long-term love that give new meaning to the phrase 'soldiering on' that we could all learn from today.

Jilly Cooper
Bisley, 1992

INTRODUCTION

Love and war are the two gigantic and timeless themes. Since history began they have been linked together by their common denominator, mankind. At first it would seem that war is all bad and love all good, but the closer you look the more you find they spill over into each other and depend on each other. In love, there can be terrifying cruelty as well as selfless devotion; in war, tenderness and passion can arise from circumstances of the most hellish depravity.

When the Imperial War Museum invited me to prepare this book, I don't think I had the smallest idea of the joy and pain it would bring. We had advertised for contributors – 'Do you have any memories of wartime romance?' – and the mail started pouring in. We were sent treasured letters and long-preserved photographs, wedding dresses, poems, love tokens; some people wrote out their memories for us, some sent poignant bundles of letters in fading copperplate. Reading through these most personal treasures was an extraordinary privilege. I was allowed to gaze into people's lives and loves, to imagine their emotions as they opened letters or wrote them, to share in their happiness or their loss. Many times I was moved to tears; often I laughed out loud. War seems to have had a hot-house effect on the flowers of love. The memories were brighter, the emotions keener, the agonies sharper. People often had to live each day as if it were their last. Love mushroomed in the strangest ways and places, between the most unlikely couples. In wartime, everyone had to try so hard – in their new roles as servicemen or women, in situations that were frightening, boring, lonely; in daily lives, where rationing bit keenly; in the face of horror, sudden attraction, injury, excitement – people had to carry on trying, and the surge of energy and emotion needed to keep going spilt over into their love affairs. To be truthful, books on wartime romance could fill the shelves of the British Library and still have lorryloads waiting in the road, so this must be just one person's anthology taken from the contributions received. It was

extremely difficult deciding how to put it into shape, but it seemed that it would work better thematically rather than historically; and within each chapter I have hopped forwards and backwards in time, dealing with subject matter rather than chronology.

Some small observations: although letter-writing is still popular today, telephones have changed dramatically the way lovers communicate with each other. If telephones had been as widespread in 1914 as they are now, we would have had only a fraction of these priceless historical documents. If typewriters had been as common and portable as their modern counterparts, we would never have seen the personal touch of handwriting or noticed the widespread standard of literacy. Without cameras, audio tapes and video cassettes, people had to rely on written thoughts and descriptions, and in doing so they may have written more honestly and fully of things that are difficult to say. Perhaps the songs *did* mean more to people in those faraway days; and yet in recent conflicts the songs people choose are still the romantic ones (with words you can hear). In our throw-away society it seems that no one would bother to keep the tiny treasures and crumpled photographs that make up so much of this book and the exhibition – but is that true, I wonder? We all still hoard little sentimental notes and knick-knacks. Distance may have lent enchantment to the scene, but perhaps the scene was rather enchanting in close-up as well.

Most of the contributions are concerned with the First and Second World Wars; this isn't surprising as they affected everyone, everywhere, for years. Modern methods of warfare have isolated conflicts, such as the Falklands War and the Gulf War (we received virtually nothing about the Falklands War). The twentieth century has produced the most durable and tangible memories of war of all time, on disc, book, film, camera and tape; but nothing can remember – or love – like the human heart.

I am indebted to Dr Christopher Dowling and the staff of the Imperial War Museum for their unfailing kindness and help, and in particular to Penny Ritchie Calder: without them, this book would not have been possible. It is dedicated to all the people who have so generously allowed me to use their stories here; and to all those absent but not forgotten whose stories do not appear because there was no room. To them all, living or departed, my gratitude and love.

OPPOSITE: Demurely modest – a typical British actress pin-up of 1914.

— 1 —
PIN-UPS

'Your sweet face seems to haunt my dreams'

Cheering the boys who are winning the war,
That's what Pin-up Girls are for.

M. Gibson, ENSA

There is no putting by that crown;
Queens you must always be;
Queens to your lovers;
Queens to your husbands and your sons;
Queens of higher mystery to the world beyond . . .

John Ruskin – *Of Queens' Gardens*

The pin-up girl represents all absent, longed-for femininity. She stands for everything worth fighting for, reminds the troops of what they left behind and what waits for them; she is the embodiment of glamour and mystique, seductive charm, niceness, warmth and perfection. Her beauty cheers the gloomiest barrack room – she is the focus of dreams and desires, a symbol of all that is happy, clean and safe in times of misery, filth and danger. Although the notion of this ideal woman has remained constant over the past eighty years, her outward appearance has changed, from demurely modest to brazenly provocative.

During the First World War, many of the women featured on postcards (then the most popular form of communication) were actresses and music-hall stars, or beauties portrayed in modest and sentimental poses. However, French magazines of the time provided a rather spicier view of desirable women, and drawings by Sager, Herouard and Fontan were collected avidly by British soldiers. Raphael Kirchner, a Viennese artist working for *La Vie Parisienne*, created what could be called the prototype pin-up girl, a slender erotic nymph, modelled on his wife, Nina. To this day the postcard is the preferred size and shape for photographs of the stars. A shift in moral standards after the Great War contributed to the change in pin-ups, and the rise of Hollywood provided screen stars to idolise. By the Second World War, the influence of Hollywood glamour on the genre was all pervasive.

Pin-ups occupied the pages of magazines like *Esquire* and *Reveille*, or appeared as cartoons like Jane of the *Daily Mirror*.

The sumptuously fantastic Varga girls were copied on to aircraft fuselages and tanks with appropriate titles – 'Delectable Doris', 'Miss Behaving' and so on. During the Korean War, 1950–53, poses became more explicit, and in the years that followed the pin ups

The art of painting the female form on to aircraft fuselages and vehicles reached its apotheosis in the Second World War and the Korean War. Some of this 'nose art' represented the wives or girlfriends of the pilot or crew. By 1989 the American *Air Force Times* reported two women pilots as saying they could be mollified 'if just one airplane had a likeness of a well-muscled, half-nude man'.

OPPOSITE: Reproductions of Raphael Kirchner's girls were in great demand during the First World War, with young officers competing to see who could collect the most.

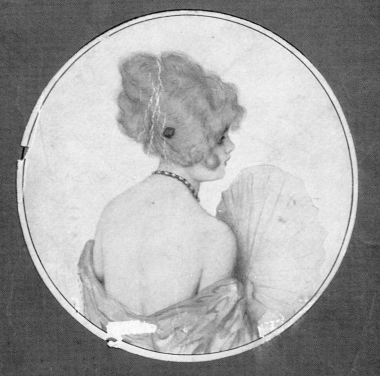

Copyright: *Bruton Galleries, Ltd., Bruton St., W.* 1

MISS RED-CAP

radiated ever more glamour – Jayne Mansfield, Ann-Margret (queen of the Vietnam War), Joan Collins, and the most loved pin-up of them all, Marilyn Monroe. During the Falklands campaign in 1982, Page 3 girls featured heavily, alongside more conventional heroines like the Princess of Wales and Selina Scott. The real split in attitude to women as pin-ups came in the recent Gulf War: although Page 3 girls were still there, the more frequently seen image was of the serviceman looking longingly at photographs of his wife, children or girlfriend. The number of women fighting alongside the men meant that an idealised reminder of femininity was no longer so important – the real thing was there. Fact and fantasy shared top billing for the first time.

OPPOSITE: **Kirchner's ethereal beauties were the first wartime pin-ups, bringing fantasy and eroticism to soldiers enduring the horrors of the trenches on the western front.**

Ken Davis, a young soldier posted overseas, kept up a cheerful friendship in letters to his pen-pal Flo. 'All I want is letters and companionship,' he remarks, before blithely suggesting a camping holiday next time he is in Blighty. Much more important to him is the loss of his favourite pin-up:

The Princess of Wales represented idealised femininity – and perhaps also a symbol of the nation – to British soldiers fighting in the Falklands conflict of 1982.

I had a terrific setback today when I returned back to my pre-fabricated dug-out and found that my home-made stove had got too hot, and my favourite pin-up girl has been burnt. Ah well, such is war. If you ever come across a picture of Betty Grable, Lamour etc, then just slip it in a letter, and once again I will sleep peacefully with Grable above my pillow.

JANE . . .

OPPOSITE & ABOVE: Jane, the *Daily Mirror* strip-cartoon heroine, started off as a Bright Young Thing. She was drawn from life by Norman Pett using Christabel Leighton-Porter as his model. The morale and effectiveness of RAF bombers on night raids over Germany depended on the state of Jane's undress in the cartoon that morning.

'I remember at the Admiralty during the war, no admiral ever settled down to his day's work until he had looked to see whether the young lady's clothes were on or off,' recalled a member of Churchill's coalition government. 'During periods of bad news the editor always kept up morale by keeping her clothes off.'

The legend grew that Jane stripped for victory. It was rumoured that the first armoured vehicle ashore on D-Day carried a picture of Jane stark naked.

These frilly knickers were worn by Christabel Leighton-Porter when she was modelling for the Jane cartoons. American forces watched Jane's antics with interest. When she did finally appear *au naturel*, a US newspaper in the Far East proclaimed 'Jane Gives All' and went on to comment, 'Well, sirs, you can go home now. Right smack out of the blue and with no one even threatening her, Jane peeled a week ago. The British 36th Division immediately gained six miles and the British attacked in the Arakan. Maybe we Americans ought to have Jane, too.'

Cherry Richards, the first official army back-page pin-up, appearing in *Soldier* magazine in August 1945. She looked glamorous, despite the fact that because of clothes rationing she had to make her swimsuit out of an old vest.

When *Soldier* magazine decided to drop their pin-up 'bird-on-the-back' in 1966, they received a mixed bag of letters, 'Bring her back' and 'We want our girls back' alternating with 'Congratulations on getting rid of the pin-ups'. It must be said the former outnumbered the latter by about forty to one. One reader suggested:

Seriously, if we're not going to get film or show-biz pin-ups, why not a Women's Royal Army Corps or Queen Alexandra's Royal Army Nursing Corps beauty each month? Let the girls know they're still appreciated in Civvy Street and perhaps boost recruiting at the same time.

Alfredo Vargas created an idealised dream woman: good-humoured and lusciously proportioned, she appeared first as the centrefold picture in *Esquire* magazine. Alfredo, having dropped the 's' from his surname, saw the celebrated Varga beauties hit the peak of their fame in 1942. At the end of the war he was awarded a citation by US President Truman for his contribution to the upkeep of forces' morale.

The tradition of official pin-ups in the forces is still very much alive today. The Royal Marine pin-up – Miss *Globe and Laurel* – is traditionally the winner of the Butlins Miss Holiday Princess competition. Sergeant Dick Stokes outlines below the duties she will be expected to perform during her year-long reign:

1. Visiting units (morale boosting)
2. Charity events
3. Increasing awareness of the Royal Marines
4. Presentations
5. Modelling for the *Globe and Laurel* magazine

During her reign she will be offered the opportunity to take part in the following:

a. Unarmed combat
b. Abseiling
c. Evasive driving
d. Driving speed boats and various landing craft
e. Free-fall parachuting
f. Firing assorted weapons
g. RM physical training
h. Assault and endurance courses

BELGIANS LIKE HER PICTURE

IN a house that was used as a rendezvous by members of the Belgian Underground Army of Resistance there hangs a photograph of a West Ham fire girl.

She is Firewoman Doreen Morrisson, of Prince Regent-lane Fire Station, Plaistow.

How the picture came into the possession of the Belgians is a mystery, but a British airman saw it hanging on the wall, and, on reading the girl's name and address on the back, wrote to her informing her of his discovery. In his letter the airman adds that the Belgian patriots greatly admired her looks.

She is the daughter of Leading Fireman W. Morrisson, of Silvertown Fire Station. She worked in an office before the war, but assisted on a farm before joining the NFS.

Firewoman Morrisson

Firewoman Doreen Morrisson unwittingly became a pin-up of the Belgian Resistance in 1944.

Michelle Egginton of Peterborough, the latest Miss *Globe and Laurel*, gets shooting practice from the Royal Marines.

OVERLEAF, LEFT: **Hugely popular from the 1890s right up until 1914, the Gibson Girl was the forerunner of the modern pin-up.**
OVERLEAF, RIGHT: **Bruce Bairnsfather's illustration for his division's 1915 Christmas card.**

The actress and singer Marlene Dietrich gave hundreds of concerts for troops, eating out of mess tins and wearing uniform while on tour. Although she worked exclusively for the Allied cause she was popular with soldiers on both sides.

Revudeville No. 138

Beatrice Appleyard, George Carden, Windmill Girls

"MOODS AND FANCIES" BAL

Not surprisingly, the chance to escape from the reality of wartime into a world of fun, glamour and music was irresistible. At the outbreak of the Second World War, however, all London theatres closed down (even the Windmill Theatre, which later stayed open throughout the Blitz). Cinemas and dance halls were also ordered to be closed, there was no television to watch and the wireless became the only source of songs and entertainment. Months passed and gradually the theatres opened again, revues and musicals

SONIA

MARGARET SMALLEY

MARGOT HARRIS

TREVES

CRYSTAL

PAT WADDINGTON

HUIA COOPER

Girls

udeville No. 133

"JUNGLE RHYTHM" BALLET

George Carden, Beatrice Appleyard, Ivor Beddoes, Windmill Girls, Revudebelles

drew in the crowds and dance halls throbbed to wild jitterbugging and jiving.

Dancing was the thing – romantic waltzes and foxtrots, the hokey cokey and the conga, the Lambeth Walk, it didn't matter as long as you could dance. But, as has always happened in times of trouble, music, and especially songs, became the enduring, heart-catching memory-makers. The more patriotic songs of the First World War gave way to unashamedly sentimental ballads, much to

People seeking entertainment in London's wartime blackout made straight for the famous Windmill Theatre. Several of the Windmill Girls married servicemen: Doreen Moore, shown here, became the wife of an RAF fighter pilot.

the despair of the higher authorities in the services and Westminster. They felt that wistful songs would produce spineless soldiers, a notion that was clearly not borne out in reality.

The Entertainments National Services Association – ENSA – provided live entertainment anywhere there were troops. Screen and stage stars in battledress worked tirelessly in war zones across Europe, North Africa and the Far East. ENSA (fondly known as Every Night Something Awful) and the American United Services Organization mobilised their battalions of comedians, actors, musicians and dancers, and in remote corners of warfare the services organised their own concert parties and camp entertainments. Music, both live and recorded, was provided by big bands, under Glenn Miller, Tommy Dorsey, Geraldo and Victor Sylvester. Crooners like Bing Crosby and Frank Sinatra and singers like Anne Shelton, Gracie Fields and Vera Lynn entertained the troops wherever they were needed. 'Lili Marlene' was the greatest soldiers' song of the Second World War. Allied troops learned it from German PoWs in the North African desert in 1941. Its theme is a soldier being separated from his sweetheart. The first verse provides an unfading snapshot of the girlfriend half illuminated by the lantern by the barrack gate, waiting patiently in the lamplight for her soldier. Ever since men first organised armies and went to fight, women have waved them goodbye and waited for them to return. 'Lili Marlene' could have been sung in the Trojan Wars or at the Battle of Waterloo.

It was a poll taken in 1940 by the BBC amongst British Expeditionary Force troops that eventually turned up the title 'the Forces Sweetheart' for Vera Lynn. She was voted the most popular singer above Deanna Durbin, Judy Garland and Bing Crosby; her instantly recognisable voice had caught the imagination and hearts of servicemen. She had an unerring instinct for picking the right songs, which she sang with an extraordinary blend of sincerity and tenderness. Before the war she had been a popular vocalist with big bands led by Billy Cotton and Charlie Kunz. She married the

Anne Rose Murphy W/179211 enlisted in 1942 – her lovely face was frequently photographed for the Ministry of Information and for services magazines.

'The Forces Sweetheart' Vera Lynn kept a tiny lucky black cat charm in this purse which she carried with her while on tour in Egypt, India and the Far East in 1944. The tour was a gruelling one, but her presence had an incalculable effect on the morale of British troops serving out there. The diary she kept in Burma records a visit to a hospital where she was given another kind of token – a bullet removed from a soldier's arm.

Marilyn Monroe, arguably *the* pin-up of them all, performed in front of thousands of American soldiers during her morale-boosting visit to Korea in January 1954. Shockwaves of excitement preceded her wherever she went. The red sequin dress was worn by Monroe in *Gentlemen Prefer Blondes*, released in 1953, which was a favourite film of troops serving in Korea.

OPPOSITE: Army magazines often carried back-page photographs of famous stars – like Lana Turner – which were torn out and stuck up on walls.

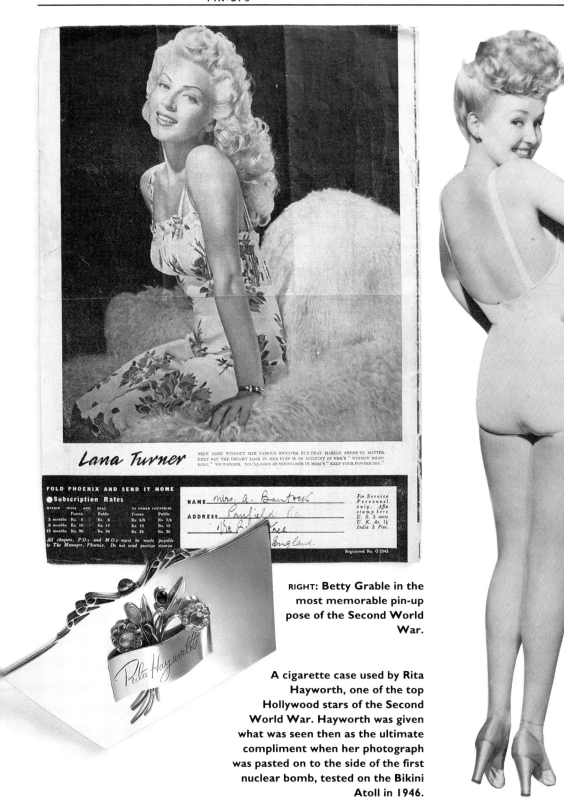

Lana Turner

SEEN HERE WITHOUT HER FAMOUS SWEATER BUT THAT HARDLY SEEMS TO MATTER. THEY SAY THE DREAMY LOOK IN HER EYES IS ON ACCOUNT OF SHE'S "WINDOW SHOPPING," WE WONDER. YOU'LL SOON BE SEEING HER IN MGM'S "KEEP YOUR POWDER DRY."

FOLD PHOENIX AND SEND IT HOME

● Subscription Rates

	INDIA AND	SEAC	TO OTHER COUNTRIES	
WITHIN	Forces	Public	Forces	Public
3 months	Rs. 5	Rs. 6	Rs. 6/8	Rs. 7/8
6 months	Rs. 10	Rs. 12	Rs. 13	Rs. 15
12 months	Rs. 20	Rs. 24	Rs. 26	Rs. 30

All cheques, P.O.s and M.O.s must be made payable to The Manager, Phoenix. Do not send postage stamps.

NAME Mrs. A. Bantock
ADDRESS Penfield Cl.
         Mr B. ... Free
         England.

For Service
Personnel
only. Affix
stamp here
U. S. 3 cents
U. K. As. 1½
India 3 Pice.

Registered No. Q 2943.

RIGHT: **Betty Grable** in the most memorable pin-up pose of the Second World War.

A cigarette case used by Rita Hayworth, one of the top Hollywood stars of the Second World War. Hayworth was given what was seen then as the ultimate compliment when her photograph was pasted on to the side of the first nuclear bomb, tested on the Bikini Atoll in 1946.

Despite being commissioned officially, this Second World War recruitment poster for the Auxiliary Territorial Service was subsequently considered to be 'unsuitable' and the 'Blonde Bombshell' drawn by Abram Games was banned; most of the posters were pulped. The model, Corinne Gardner, was in her teens when she sat for the artist. Games had been briefed to come up with a design that would attract more women to join the ATS, but the use of lipstick was criticised by an MP in a debate in the House of Commons.

Tom Roberts, serving with the Royal Marines, was frequently mistaken for the Hollywood swashbuckler and screen idol Errol Flynn.

clarinettist and saxophonist Harry Lewis when they were both working for the bandleader Ambrose. Vera Lynn herself has never worked out exactly how or when the magic began to work, but the facts show that request programmes began to be swamped with letters asking for her songs, and by 1941, a radio programme featuring her had been aired. It was called *Sincerely Yours* and became a huge success, aimed as it was at 'the men of the Forces – a letter in words and music – from Vera Lynn, accompanied by

Fred Hartley and his music. A sentimental presentation by Howard Thomas'.

The three songs she is most remembered for are 'Yours', the love song, 'We'll Meet Again', the optimistic song, and 'The White Cliffs of Dover', the patriotic song. Vera Lynn became the girl next door, the big sister, the universal fiancée, and her songs were greetings cards from servicemen to their sweethearts and back again. Her handling of quite ordinary, commercial songs gave them an intimate intensity, and what she sang was what the troops wanted. When Basil Dean, who organised ENSA, asked her where she would be prepared to go on concert tours she replied, 'Where I can do most good and where not many performers go.' 'That's easy,' he said, 'Burma.'

Vera and her accompanist Len Edwards set off on 24 March 1944, on a two-and-a-half-month tour which was rigorous by any standards: Cairo, Basra, Bombay, Calcutta, Chittagong, and then Burma itself, doing two or three shows a day, sometimes performing in front of a few men, sometimes in front of thousands. The conditions were spartan in the extreme: buckets to wash in, bed bugs, floods, journeys on roads no more than tracks, eight to ten hours' travel a day. They took with them a battered upright piano, a microphone and a primitive public-address system. Men slogged in from miles around in full battle kit, prepared to wait all day to hear the Forces Sweetheart sing to them. She visited grisly field hospitals, sometimes three in a morning, then sang at an afternoon show and after that, at an evening concert. As often as she could she changed from her ENSA uniform into a pink dress which grew sodden with sweat during the performances. She kept a diary, knowing it was forbidden. She nevertheless made short entries every day in pencil, all too often noting 'worn out', 'exhausted again'. In one remote camp she remembers meeting some of the Chindits, Wingate's legendary crack troop Special Force, which operated in unbelievable danger behind

In 1944 in the summer fields of France, the Normandy Nomads were inspired by a pin-up on the side of their wireless truck. Deprived of any feminine company, they wrote to *Lilliput* magazine with a view to forming a liaison with the charming lady in the photograph: 'I remember we likened her to an English rose and asked if we could write to her in her little country cottage where we pictured her living. We sent her a copy of our Section photograph, taken just before D-Day – I would admit we were a lecherous-looking lot.'
This is the 'shattering' reply they received: they did not feel encouraged to pursue the matter further.

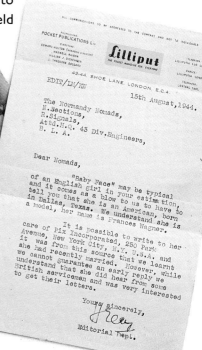

ADOLPH TREIDLER

"My girl's a WOW"

WOMAN ORDNANCE WORKER

ORDNANCE DEPARTMENT • U. S. ARMY ✸ KEEP 'EM SHOOTING

the Japanese lines. They had just emerged from months in the jungle, and needed to be deloused and cleaned before they met her.

At last it was time to turn and retrace their path – through India and the Middle East, to Britain. The day they arrived home was 6 June 1944 – D-Day, the day of the Allied invasion of Europe.

Vera Lynn was made a Dame of the British Empire in the New Year's Honours List in 1975. Her informal title, however, may eventually prove to be the more enduring: 'the Forces Sweetheart'.

Poppy Hambly and the girls she worked with in a local laundry were tired of hearing the same few records played time and again over the loudspeakers.

We girls donated tuppence from our wages every Friday to a gramophone fund. From then on we purchased all the hits of the day and the laundry rang to Vera Lynn's 'White Cliffs of Dover', 'When the Lights Go On Again' and, of course, 'We'll Meet Again'. Then there was Anne Shelton, Billy Cotton, Bing Crosby, Frank Sinatra and the rest. We loved them all. I sometimes think we wouldn't have got through the war years without them.

She was a Wren – he was her pen-friend in the RAF. He sent her a bikini from Belgium for 'a pin-up snap' and carried this photograph with him for two years before they met. Two years after that they were married in uniform on leave. Mr and Mrs Scott are still happily married today.

OPPOSITE: The image of woman as more than just a pin-up was an important propaganda tool for the Allies who were keen to encourage women to work in munitions factories and other vital wartime industries.

Photographs of girlfriends and wives were kept in all sorts of guises by men at the fighting front. Here a picture has been put beneath the grip-plate of a pistol.

Patience Strong, indefatigable writer of comforting and philosophical verses, also had the knack of perceiving anxieties and sweet memories. Many found solace and friendly advice in the short poems published in her Quiet Corner. In 'Theme Song' she echoes the sentiment expressed by Noel Coward: 'Strange how potent cheap music is.'

I've forgotten half the words, but I can still recall –
Every note of that sweet song, the sweetest song of all . . .
In the tale of our romance that tune has played a part –
The tune that's threaded through my dreams and written on my heart.

Strange that it should mean so much, that simple melody –
Running like a golden thread through every memory . . .
The theme song of our happiness, and of my love for you.
When you hear it, dearest one, do you remember too?

Helen Coleman's soothing tones on the BBC provided a much-needed morale-booster.

BBC Copyright   HELEN COLEMAN

One soldier, Sergeant Ted Cope, serving with the Eighth Army in North Africa, wrote enthusiastically to his wife of

. . . the arrival of Leslie Henson with a concert party composed entirely of well-known names . . . Vivien Leigh, Beatrice Lillie and about 5 others. I saw them the last night they were on in a Tripoli theatre. The show lasted about 2 hours and it was excellent from start to finish. It was better than any show I'd seen in England, containing as it did all top notchers, and also as we only see a show every now and then we appreciate them more.

Helen Coleman became a BBC Forces Announcer in 1944 after a hair-raising escape from Malaya just before the fall of Singapore. Although her husband was still a prisoner of war in the Far East no trace of her anxiety appeared in her voice as she introduced the radio programmes, prompting this letter from one of her many admirers:

Last night I was sitting in my mess tent all alone absolutely thoroughly browned off – which is not a very surprising fact considering that I've been in this god-forsaken country for 3 years. Before me I had my

35

SPECIAL FALKLANDS EDITION

KNAVE

GOOD LUCK AND
BEST WISHES
TO ALL OF YOU
FROM ALL OF US

AND AS SOON AS
SHE'S GOT THE
HANG OF HER
UNIFORM –
A BIG KISS FROM
OUR COVER GIRL!

This special edition of *Knave* magazine was rushed to the troops about to embark for the Falklands.

OPPOSITE: Meetings in wartime were affairs of chance – men and women were thrown together by caprices of time, place and circumstance.

monthly issue of whisky but even that for once did not dispel the feeling of boredom and general feeling of downheartedness which it normally does. Well, I decided to switch on the old radio and the first thing I heard was you announcing yourself and reading the summary of the programmes to follow. Somehow my whole outlook was changed immediately, and believe me I felt quite bucked. I don't know whether it was your voice alone (being British) or your general personality but that is my reason for writing, and I want to thank you sincerely for the job you did last night. Tonight I shall listen for you again . . .

An impromptu dance in an unorthodox setting created a vivid memory for Wren Biddy Pledge. She was travelling to the Mulberry Harbour at Arromanches:

We had only just made our way back to our cabins when a deputation of sailors came to say that we were invited to an entertainment in their mess. There a wondrous band was set up – saucepan drums, saucepan lid cymbals, combs wrapped in tissue and a rather shaky 'string section'. They immediately struck up with a lively Scots reel and then a lovely and unforgettable thing happened. In the faint glow of the blacked-out ship, a hatch heaved up in the middle of the deck and an enormous stoker slowly heaved himself out on deck. He was stripped to the waist and covered with black dust and a huge white grin split on his blackened face. He started to move – he was graceful as most big men are, and before he had done more than a few steps, our shy, retiring Scotswoman had dashed to take her place opposite him, uttering a most un-Wrenlike 'Hoch'. They danced together, faster and faster as the band egged them on, performing the most intricate and beautiful patterns until they both sank exhausted to the deck while we applauded wildly and begged for more. However, the evening ended with community singing, the inevitable finale being 'She'll be coming round the mountain when she comes'. When even the sailors had run out of ever more extraordinary improvisations on what she was doing/saying, we all went happily to bed.

— 2 —
MEETINGS

'For suddenly I saw you there . . .'

'Tisn't beauty, so to speak, nor good talk necessarily.
It's just *it*. Some women'll stay in a man's memory if
they once walked down a street.

Rudyard Kipling — *Traffics and Discoveries*

The extraordinary circumstances of wartime provided every imaginable kind of opportunity to meet new people from widely differing backgrounds. They met by letter, in hospitals, in air-raid shelters, at dance halls: they met because they worked together, rescued each other, spoke on telephones or passed signals to and fro. They met fellow servicemen's sisters, they tumbled over in bomb blasts and literally fell in love. From 1939, for the first time ever for some, there was the chance to meet Canadians, Americans, Australians, New Zealanders, Poles, Italians, Germans, French, Belgians, Dutch, in or out of uniform; and the great sweep of Commonwealth troops, from India, the Far East and Africa. Since the First World War, the rigid codes of morality and social behaviour had begun to relax, and it was easier for men and women to treat each other as equals. They worked side by side and the common enemy forged bonds between people whose paths may never have crossed in peacetime. Some were spurred on to romance by a heightened sense of danger and excitement; some spoke of a feeling of what-the-hell, it's now or never. Inhibitions faded, people escaped from the social cubby-hole life had consigned them to and behaved as they felt, rather than as they were expected to behave.

Proximity played a large part in wartime love affairs and love at first sight was not at all unusual. Psychologists say that it's our subconscious that falls in love and it only takes a few seconds. Love at first sight is not as ridiculous as some people think.

Christopher Portway, escaping from a German PoW camp in 1944, was befriended by a Czech family who hid him overnight in a cave in the hillside. The daughter Anna arrived the next day with some provisions packed in the basket on the front of her bicycle. Portway was captivated at once:

I watched every movement of her lips, every change of expression on her face as if mesmerised. She appeared younger than eighteen but self-assured with it and she held herself erect like a soldier; a real soldier, not a prisoner. She bent over to adjust the position of her bicycle pedals and I noticed her legs were strong and smooth in the weak sun. Her neck had a contrasting fairness below the fall of her dark hair.

Christopher Portway's extraordinary story is told in full in his own book *Czechmate*: he was recaptured and returned to the prison camp; after the war, unable to forget Anna, he made persistent

perilous journeys across the Iron Curtain to find her and eventually bring her back to England and marry her.

A nineteen-year-old ATS volunteer remembers 15 September 1940:

It was Battle of Britain Day and I was walking along the Great West Road from my billet, during an alert, to go on duty at Cavalry Barracks, Hounslow, London. I was very much aware of a devastatingly handsome young airman who was approaching me at full speed, but I could not understand why he was shouting, 'Get down, get down!' Before I could ask him politely what he meant, he had thrown himself at me in a typical rugger tackle and kept me pinned to the ground. Within seconds, the earth shook as a bomb exploded close by and after the shock waves had passed, he helped me to my feet, revealing a large hole in the knee of my stocking. Being the perfect gentleman, however, he apologised and invited me out the following night, and we became engaged. Five weeks later we were married.

It was a lasting and happy union which produced two sons and three grandchildren.

Another kind of explosive chance encounter introduced a young student, Margo, to Bob Pearce Carey. She was reading chemistry at Bradford College, half of which had been given over to the military. One morning, one of the professor's wives, brewing coffee for 'the dear boys', asked Margo to help light the capricious ancient boiler. It blew back and the explosion knocked her off her feet and into the strong arms of 'a shining blond Adonis' who just happened to open the door. Margo's eyelashes and hair were singed; she stammered her thanks and escaped to clean up. A week later her Adonis, who had been teaching the radar technicians, asked her to go boating on the river and they were married by special licence three months later.

Just one look at a photograph made such an impact on a young soldier travelling to the Middle East on a troop ship that he asked the friend who had showed it to him if he could keep it. He carried the little snapshot with him all through the Middle East campaign, finally plucking up the courage to write to the girl in the picture. Two years later, in November 1943, he returned to England to prepare for the Normandy landings and during that Christmas leave he was invited by the young woman's family to spend three days over the New Year with them. So at last they met face to face

– and before the train left on the third morning they decided to marry. Before their wedding, they had only spent a total of four days together; afterwards their marriage lasted for forty-six happy years.

Through an unpromising start as a Land Army girl, Mrs Bettam met her future husband:

As a domestic servant, with a slightly deformed left arm, I knew that in 1939 it was going to be impossible for me to join any of the Forces, but on making enquiries I found that as long as one was healthy & willing, the Land Army wasn't too fussy about such things as a deformed left arm. I enlisted in Midhurst in Sussex and after a quick medical was accepted without any trouble. Within a week or two I was sent to a farm near Chichester where I was to meet another green recruit like myself. Our home for the month was a Nissen hut in the corner of the farm; all it contained was two camp beds, two small chests of drawers, a table & two chairs & a calor gas stove. The utensils consisted of 3 cracked cups, 3 plates, two old saucepans plus a frying pan that had seen its best days long before we were born. We were both 16 and full of British spirit. Our uniforms were waiting for us at the farm & we had great fun fitting them on.

Nellie was a very small girl & I was 5 ft 10 and big with it, our things didn't fit either of us so we had to wait a further two weeks for the right fitting clothes to arrive, so we had to start work the first morning at 6am in our ordinary clothes and beg our food from the farm until we could get our ration books changed in order to shop at the local shop. We lived mostly on eggs that we pinched from the hens while the boss wasn't looking.

Nellie volunteered to do the dairy work on the farm & I was just to be a general worker. For the first three days all I had to do was clear what seemed to me to be miles & miles of great tall stinging nettles. I was given a scythe & a sickle & shown how to do the job & just left to get on with it. I was stung by nettles from head to foot & my dress was just one wet green mess & somehow the end of the day came.

Nellie hadn't fared much better than myself for she had been kicked over by an aggressive cow, her clothes were soiled beyond recognition & we both limped home to our little hut to wash in a tin bowl & to eat our only meal of the day given to us by the farmer, a tin of beans & half a loaf of bread. We had been given a cup of tea & a sandwich at lunch time but we went to bed pretty fed up & very hungry.

The next day was no different, I by now had got used to the scythe & wasn't too badly stung and Nellie seemed to be on better terms with her

cows. When work finished that night we dashed home & got washed & changed, & set off for the village pub where we got a decent meal & bought some food off the landlady. We also had a great evening with the local soldiers who were stationed just outside the village. They were the Irish Guards who had just come back from rescuing the Dutch Royal Family. I met John who was later to become my husband.

'I have been in the RAF 1 year today,' wrote Pilot Officer Denis Wissler on 10 July 1940. The diary was small and his daily accounts were sometimes quite brief: 'Back from leave – damn Hitler', 'Heavy flying day – met Margret, a WAAF'. On 24 September he was shot, injured and sent to hospital, where the bullet was dug out of his arm. He was given seven days' sick leave to start on Monday 30 September. The day before, Sunday 29, the diary entry reads:

Did nothing during the day but there was the usual band in the Mess and when they packed up I completed the party at the Sergeants' Mess. Met Edith Heap and fell in love with her at sight. I rather cut Margret Cameron

Pilot Officer Denis Wissler's diary records the moment he met and fell in love with Edith Heap. They became engaged shortly afterwards and began making plans for their marriage. Six weeks after their first meeting his aircraft was shot down over the North Sea and he was never seen again.

OPPOSITE: **The occasional evening out came as a welcome distraction from the drabness and austerity of wartime Britain. Dances and social events also provided an ideal opportunity for men and women to meet. Men required only a slick of Brylcreem and a well-pressed uniform, but women had to use greater ingenuity to achieve a glamorous look. Instead of thick Utility stockings, legs were dyed and seams drawn on with an eyebrow pencil; black lace might be added to an old day-dress for a more sophisticated evening style; and, with cosmetics rationed to a mere quarter of pre-war supplies, lipstick had to be mixed with cold cream as a subsitute for rouge. A favourite scent was Bourjois's 'Evening in Paris'; even now, fifty years on, the lingering fragrance from the little blue bottle conjures up the headiness of wartime dance halls.**

and I am not so popular with her as I was!!!

Edith Heap takes up the story in her account, written later:

We got on like a house on fire . . . he made a beeline for me and we danced the rest of the evening. I was bowled over and Denis & I arranged to write each day and meet again as soon as our duties allowed it.

Edith was a bomber and fighter plotter in the Operations Room at Debden:

I had a grid map with tracing paper over it – one for each sortie, & was connected to our own Direction Finding Station & told the plots of our fighters. Winifred watched the bomber plots on the board and put their track on the paper in a different colour. Each plot had to have its time alongside, so that the battle taking place could be followed & reviewed by the powers that be.

Denis and Edith, on a forty-eight-hour leave, went to Cambridge. He had scribbled in his diary, 'My God, it seems to be the real thing this time. She is so sweet and seems to like me as much as I like her.' He was in two minds about how his parents would react – he loved them dearly and didn't want to do anything improper that might hurt them – but concluded in his diary:

They did it themselves when they were the same age as me.

Edith:

We couldn't get in at the Garden House, he came out saying, 'They only had a double room. I said no. That was right, wasn't it?' 'Yes,' I said & I wondered later whether he would have asked me to marry him if I had said no. Anyway we got into the Red Lion at Trumpington, oh place of sublime happiness. Had dinner & lots of chat – then it was getting late. Denis came upstairs with me, & asked me to marry him. 'Yes', of course, and he ordered a bottle of champagne, which the hotelier brought up and wished us well. I was surprised that he didn't say anything about Denis being in my room – definitely not done in those days. But he needn't have worried: after all the bubbly we retired to our respective beds!

The next day Denis drove her to London to meet his parents, having telephoned to tell them he was bringing a friend. Edith became more and more apprehensive as the car approached Dolphin Square:

DANCE PROGRAMME.

ADELPHI HOTEL (Roof Garden)

1st February 1941.

R. A. F. SQDN.
TENGAH.

... and when we got there I was in a blue funk – all down the corridor and then standing outside the door. Denis held my hand to give us both courage and rang the bell. Shouts of welcome & Denis shot me into the bathroom (just inside the door) while he told them the news. I just stood there shaking in my shoes. A yell from the sitting room & I emerged to be hugged and kissed – I belonged to the family from that minute.

Denis and Edith returned to their bases, Denis to Ipswich, Edith to Debden. They met when they could, on compassionate leave, to plan their wedding. They decided on 4 January, his parents' wedding anniversary.

Then came 11 November. Edith wrote:

Our squadrons were in the thick of it & just before we came off watch at 1200 hours there was a cry of 'Blue 4 going down into the sea'.

Officially they didn't know who it was. But Edith did, although, paralysed with shock, she wouldn't admit it. Later it was confirmed: Denis was missing, no parachute and, as the days dragged by, no hope.

He and Edith had known each other barely six weeks.

At the start of the 1939–45 war, Radio Direction Finding operators were mostly men, usually engineers and scientists. As the war went on more and more WAAFs were recruited to RDF or radar, as it was later called. When their sensitive tracking equipment became worn or inaccurate through constant scanning of the screens and movement of the gonio knob, the operator would call a mechanic.

To assess the trouble he would have to come close beside her in the low light of the receiver room to peer into the tube, perhaps overlay his hand on hers. He would have to operate the set with her and under the pressure of the real-time war situation they would be united in a mutual problem until it was solved.

No wonder that many friendships and enduring marriages ensued between WAAF operators and RDF mechanics, and who knows how many lifetimes together started from that physical contact? WAAFs were also trained as electricians. Wendy Webster went to work at RAF Lindholme.

We were met with absolute hostility. Until then only men had been doing our jobs and they laughed at us women in our big dungarees climbing up and seeing to the generators. Their language was terrible and they'd pull

our legs and say, 'Come on, we'll show you the golden rivet' – that was to get you into the cockpit and have their wicked way, I suppose. There was such glamour attached to Spitfire pilots and terrific rivalry with the ground crew. The air crew had priority over everything, including sex. There was this feeling that they lived for the moment, so if a WAAF went with one of the air crew then it was definitely a body and soul job – he wanted the lot because he was a pilot and might not be here tomorrow.

Women had to get used to the cool reception that often greeted them in their new positions of authority in the services. ATS on the guns and working searchlights, Wrens on Aldis lamps and as wireless operators, women doing men's work were occasionally seen as ridiculous and insulting by men – but the hostile reactions soon died down, and women who had hitherto only been acceptable as nurses, factory workers and waitresses became an indispensable link further up the chain of command.

Dear Doc, waited till 3 but no signs – if you still want to go to Blomberg – I'll be at the mess! Oscar.

She wasn't called Doc, she was called Marjorie and his name was really David Barr: Oscar was his current nickname. He had spied her entering the mess in Detmold, Germany . . .

. . . with three very senior officers indeed – lieutenant-generals at the very least – the loveliest girl I have ever seen. She was dressed in the smart, eye-catching uniform of an American army captain. I turned to my mates and said, 'That's the lady I'm going to marry!'

He sent her a message saying she would be meeting her future husband when she met him and asked if he might take her to Blomberg, where she worked with her UNRRA team in a hospital. Reluctantly she agreed. After waiting half an hour for her on the day, 'Oscar' got cold feet and scribbled the note, putting it on the table in the mess. As he was turning to leave, the note was taken from his hand – her ambulance had broken down and she had only arrived at that moment. They were engaged a week later and married within two months. Forty-six years later that scrap of paper is a treasured relic.

Captain FC Saxon, wounded in the First World War and recovering in hospital, was mobile enough to assist with bedpans:

It was usual, in the Ward, for all of us to do what we could to help the

Nurses; and we who could walk at all used to help those who could not, by taking things to the Sluice Room.

We even used to 'wait upon' an ex-RSM who had been commissioned 'in the field'; in spite of his keeping us awake with his perpetual 'canteen' song,

> And a little child shall lead them,
> Lead them gently on their way,
> And shall guide them straight to heave-ern,
> Lest they ever try to stray

and so on, for a number of verses, before the poor fellow went himself to sleep. Being all in a strong nasal tone, it was not easily forgotten (I remember it after over fifty years).

A memory I have of the 2nd London Hospital (which was a converted girls' school) concerned a visit of the local dignitaries.

I had just collected the wherewithal from a patient at the far end of the Ward, properly covered (as was the custom in those days) with a napkin, when at the opposite end entered the 'party', led by the woman Mayor.

Now, was I to advance in the hope of reaching the Sluice Room, which was mid-way; or retreat to the bed? I decided on the former; but as I advanced, so did the lady.

I picked up a bunch of flowers from a centre table, to disguise what I was carrying, and continued my advance.

Seeing the flowers, however, made the Lady Mayor think that I was about to present her with a bouquet, and so as I went forward so did she, leaving her party yards behind.

I got to the middle first, fortunately, and turned towards the Sluice, where I stayed until the party had left.

In the Hospital, what I chiefly remember, however, is the girl who came to visit the chap in the next bed.

That is another story, for she ultimately became Mrs Saxon.

Norman Thomas, attending a dance at Dover Town Hall in October 1943, spotted an attractive blonde girl across the floor. The band struck up a waltz and he walked over to ask her to dance. Halfway there the lights went out – it was a 'black-out waltz'. When the lights came on again he found he was dancing with a brunette in WAAF uniform: she was in 'B' crew, RAF Swingate, working in air-sea rescue from a Nissen hut on the cliffs. By January they were married.

Some encounters left a lasting impression even if they didn't have a romantic ending. Second Officer Rosemary Keyes, a Wren

The admiring patients of Doris Benjamin, a young VAD nurse at a military hospital in Oxfordshire, used to give her shoulder flashes from their uniforms which she sewed into her cape while off duty.

working under Admiral Ramsay at Dover, was on night duty with another cypher officer when an exhausted, unshaven and unknown young naval officer appeared in the doorway of the cypher office.

'I believe you have an armchair, may I borrow it? My boss says I can have an hour's sleep.' Of course we said yes, but offered a very uncomfortable bed, a folding iron affair in the corner of the office. 'No, thank you, this is wonderful,' he said, falling into the large leather armchair and falling asleep immediately. I covered him up with our one rug, and he slept motionless, quite undisturbed by the clatter of the typewriter, our voices as we worked and the noise of fresh cyphers being brought to our hatch. At about 4 a.m. the work had stopped temporarily and I lay upon the awful iron bed and went fast asleep, to be wakened by our unknown guest covering me up with the rug. He then vanished and we never saw him again or ever discovered who he was or where he had come from.

Just as roses continued to bloom beside the trenches, so love was born even in the most dreadful circumstances. Jim Wheeler's regiment, a Light Field Ambulance, was sent into Belsen to liberate the concentration camp, an experience he describes as beyond comprehension. They established a mess in a marquee in an open field outside the camp and carpeted and furnished it with material from the SS officers' quarters in the camp. Some Hungarian PoWs, kept on as orderlies servicing baths, provided the regiment with regular hot water which, after living rough since the Normandy landings, was luxury indeed.

The 'horror camp' had been burned down ceremonially before a general hospital arrived a fortnight later to nurse, succour and prepare the surviving inmates for evacuation. Upon arrival, three VADs, searching for old five-gallon petrol tins to use as washbasins, were introduced to the mess, where they were entertained to drinks, also liberated from the SS quarters. Jim and one of the VADs, Mary, were attracted at once, but were concerned that the emotional factors generated by the situation might be distorting the amount of real affection they felt for each other. They agreed upon an unbinding engagement to marry, promising to meet in England as soon as possible in a less emotionally charged atmosphere.

They did meet again, but only after Jim's regiment had spent some months in Norway. When they met, they realised their feelings were unchanged and they married in March 1946. Forty-six years later, with children and grandchildren, Jim writes, possibly

recalling the stark horror of Belsen, 'We are so fortunate.'

The friendly GI invasion of Britain started off a series of shock waves which continue to reverberate today. Into damp, poor, dimly lit, heavily rationed little Britain rolled wave after wave of tall, well-dressed, comparatively rich, exuberant, gum-chewing, classless American soldiers. At a time when morale was at its lowest, when many of Britain's young men were overseas fighting, the GIs appeared to be sent from heaven, with their movie-star voices, jitterbugging skills and passion for 'dames'. Just before the invasion of France, there were estimated to be over a million GIs in Britain and the female population by and large was bowled over. For many people in Britain it was the first time they had had a chance to meet a black person, and though at the time the US army was virtually segregated, over here black GIs were generally welcomed as equals and, by many accounts, often preferred as boyfriends.

We find the coloured troops much nicer to deal with . . .

a canteen worker from Hull is reported as saying.

. . . in canteen life and such, we like serving them, they are always so courteous and have a very natural charm that most whites miss.

Everybody adores the Negro troops . . .

The Negroes are very polite and much smarter.

The girls really go for them in preference to the white boys, a fact that irks the boys no end.

Black or white, the Americans were welcomed with relief and excitement by women, married and unmarried (and often under age). Thousands became GI brides, sailing away to a land hitherto only seen on the movies which in reality sometimes fell far short of their dreams. Thousands more had illegitimate babies, and either had them adopted, absorbed them into their families or passed them off as being the children of their British husbands. Illegal backstreet abortions took place, posing a serious danger to both patient and doctor, who risked being struck off. Society shunned the single mother, but for bored, lonely soldiers far from home and young girls starved of romance, unplanned parenthood and the threat of VD were the last things on their minds.

OPPOSITE: **American GIs began arriving in Britain in 1942. They were each given a copy of this booklet to help them understand the strange customs and quirks that prevailed in this country. It also provided hints on how to acknowledge British servicewomen.**

17th August 1943.

HMS Mercury I, Haslemere.

Our daily papers are plastered with advertisements on venereal disease because it's becoming a national menace. Women's magazines are full of articles exhorting girls to live cleanly. The number of illegitimate children being born is so great that Parliament is fighting about marriage by proxy. There are more prostitutes in London now than ever before. Even society girls are joining their ranks . . .

wrote Maureen Bolster to her husband-to-be, Eric Wells.

Do you know what the Yanks are saying now? They're saying that Englishwomen are the most immoral in the world. Nice, isn't it?

And I'm really beginning to think it's true. Coming down on the train opposite me were an American army officer and an attractive, well-dressed girl of the upper classes. They were sitting hand in hand and talking about the hotel they'd been staying in. They didn't look in the least married. When she made a neat little joke about her husband being at sea and what the eye didn't see, I felt rather sick.

There were, of course, members of the public who felt that the best way to deal with the Americans was to leave them severely alone. They had different uniforms, accents and attitudes, and were probably dangerous. The American Red Cross set up clubs for their soldiers, small havens for homesick servicemen, with American flags on the walls and American music on the radiogram. British girls enrolled as hostesses, whose job was to circulate among the men, chatting and dancing. There were games rooms, quiet corners for letter-writing, piano lounges, bars and ballrooms for the Saturday night hop. One hostess, writing of a colleague, remembers:

Out on the town – GI Edward Bednarcik's passes permitting him an evening in London. On the reverse are the warnings: 'Do not buy your liquor from strangers or cheap private clubs. DO NOT flash a roll of money.'

She was an attractive girl, though a little on the plump side, with dark hair and eyes, and creamy skin.

It did not take her long to find herself a regular boyfriend, but I wondered what she saw in this particular soldier, who seemed to me to be about as exciting as a piece of wood.

'What's he like?' I asked her one day.

'All right,' she replied, non-committally.

A SHORT GUIDE TO

GREAT BRITAIN

WAR AND NAVY DEPARTMENTS
Washington, D. C.

g to be careful about—if you are invited into
ome and the host exhorts you to "eat up—
ty on the table," go easy. It may be the fam-
s for a whole week spread out to show their
y.

eans Lives. It is always said that Americans
ore food into their garbage cans than any other
eats. It is true. Most British food is imported even in
nation. We have always been a "pro-
imes, and for the last two years the British have
taught not to waste the things that their ships bring
om abroad. British seamen die getting those convoys
ough. The British have been taught this so thoroughly
t they now know that gasoline and food represent the
es of merchant sailors. And when you burn gasolin
eedlessly, it will seem to them as if you are wasting t
lood of those seamen—when you destroy or waste fo
you have wasted the life of another sailor.

British Women At War. A British woman officer or
commissioned officer can—and often does—give ord
a man private. The men obey smartly and know it i
shame. For British women have proven themselves in this
war. They have stuck to their posts near burning ammunition dumps, delivered messages afoot after their motor-
cycles have been blasted from under them. They have
pulled aviators from burning planes. They have died at

23

the gun posts and as they fell another girl has stepped
directly into the position and "carried on." There is not
a *single record* in this war of any British woman in uni-
formed service quitting her post or failing in her duty
under fire.

Now you understand why British soldiers respect the
women in uniform. They have won the right to the
utmost respect. When you see a girl in khaki or air-force
blue with a bit of ribbon on her tunic—remember she
didn't get it for knitting more socks than anyone else in
Ipswich.

RSUS AMERICAN

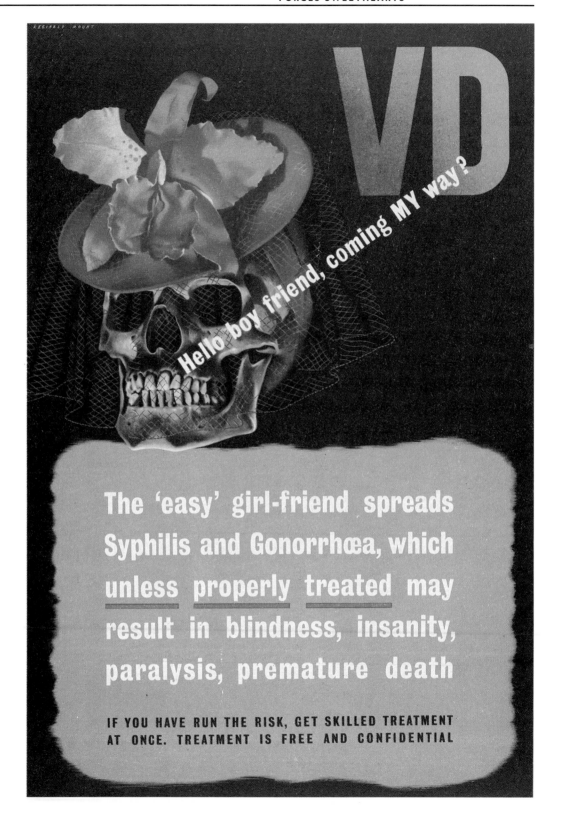

'No, well, I mean – he doesn't seem to be your type. Does he take you out and give you a good time?'

'It depends on what you call a good time,' she said evasively.

'Well, where *does* he take you?'

'To the college – to the kitchens.'

'Good Lord! Whatever for?'

But I might have guessed, though the reason had not yet occurred to me.

Then came the confession.

'He cooks for the army, but he was a chef before. I get lovely meals at the college.'

There were lashings of everything, she explained; food that we were short of such as steak, chicken, beef, pork, gammon, bacon, lamb and sausages were all served up with the appropriate trimmings.

A young munitions worker never forgot the friendly GI she met in Lancashire. She lived a cloistered life, only going out to work the long hours at the factory. Her friend Joan persuaded her to take a day off in Manchester, a train ride from her home. They had heard that 'a lot was going on in Manchester'.

Was I surprised when my friend and I got off the train at Manchester.

The streets were crowded and Joan my friend was very smart and could take care of herself. She took me down near the Midland Hotel and lots of American Service Men were coming off the train that had come in from Warrington.

They all seemed happy and friendship seemed to be what they wanted, a few crooked their left arm and asked me to grab hold and walk out with them. I just smiled and carried on with my friend. Joan wanted to go dancing so she walked past a cinema, the 'Odeon', turned off to the 'Ritz' ballroom the main one in Manchester. She suddenly said Mary! someone is shouting for you. I was so shy and nervous. I turned round very quickly and a dapper energetic five foot seven American was begging me to keep him company, he seemed kind. I looked and quickly said I am very sorry do not come to town very often, work very long hours nights and days. He was looking right into my eyes. He pleaded. Please would you like to accompany me to a British film. It's Emily Bronte's book; they made a film *Jane Eyre*. When I agreed he immediately paid for Joan to go dancing in the Ritz Ballroom, made her comfortable and escorted me to the new cinema built just before nineteen-forty (the Gaumont) – it was cosy and he was a gentleman, such good company and very straightforward, I was not afraid of him. Most of the servicemen we met respected him, he was a decent good living person. He begged me to give him my address. He came

OPPOSITE: **In 1943–44 the growing concern about looser morals led the Ministry of Health to promote a national campaign warning of the dangers of venereal disease.**

and my mother thought he was a very nice person. They got on very well indeed, in fact he brought her lots of things; eatables. Like a small boy he piled them in the centre of the eating table. I think he wanted a friendly home, he also went in to all the neighbours, they loved him, honestly, everyone took to him. He took me out to dinner and got all the English soldiers in the cafe to sit round our table and asked them if they minded and said you know our pay is better, please enjoy your meal. It was steak and vegetables. He was as I have said, a Good Clean friendly person. Yes! he went home because he wrote me a few times, alas I had married and my husband wrote in answer to the last letter. My sister brought them and instead of giving the letters to me gave them to my husband.

A touchingly innocent proposal of marriage received by a Land Army girl from an Italian prisoner of war who had been sent to work on the same farm in Wiltshire. After 1945 a significant number of British women married former Italian or German PoWs whom they had met during the war.

When Dorothy Robertson WRNS was a Petty Officer, there were only a hundred girls on board ship with her and five or six thousand servicemen, so their daily meetings with the men were 'rationed': different batches were allowed up on 'B' deck every day, with dancing on deck at night. She remembers vividly waiting in convoy to enter the Suez Canal:

It was gloriously hot and sunny and the sea had that smooth greenish tinge all around. We were up on B Deck with lots of the lads, looking over the side watching ship movements and generally wondering what was going to happen next . . . when we began to notice that a lot of landing craft seemed to be moving towards us, filled with men in white helmets. I shall never forget, as they came alongside, far below, one helmet looked upwards at us on deck and emitted a loud cry, 'Gee! Dames!' Whereupon the whole flotilla of landing craft looked up and bawled, 'Gee! Dames!' – We girls simply fled down to our cabins and locked ourselves in . . . In subsequent days, the Yanks were rationed to meet us, like all the other troops, but somehow or other they seemed to appear here and there on our deck in spite of this, and I must say, they were often very amusing, and, of course, terrible flirts. Our British lads were absolutely furious and used to surround us, 3 or 5 to one Wren, as an anti-Yank bodyguard, whenever they could, from then onwards. We also had a contingent of ANZACs on board at Suez, on their way home after fighting in North Africa. The New Zealanders were more polite than the Aussies, and they were all very friendly and surprised to see women on the troopship.

Before he was called up in May 1940 Charles Gerrard had been a printer. Now with the Royal Artillery and the Royal Signals he was travelling abroad for the first time, to Cape Town and India, Iraq, Egypt and Tunisia. He and Lily wrote regularly to each other. It was in Italy that he was profoundly touched by the effects of starvation on ordinary people, particularly the women:

You may not believe me, dear, but I've seen a lot of terrible things since leaving home and of course Italy took the prize. I've seen women and girls – some women with innumerable children – selling themselves for something to eat while their husbands had to turn their heads.

We once saw a very pretty young girl – probably never been touched before – running home half crying and half laughing – naturally she had committed the crime for a loaf of bread – laughing because she never had anything to eat for two days and crying because maybe her life was ruined. And yet the Italians are one of the finest races I've seen in all my travels – beat the English –

There, Mama is the head of the house and normally young ladies are never out unescorted.

If it had come home to England and you'd been one of the victims – how would I face it? Hunger is the worst pain of all. Hanging around encampments is their life – sending their brothers on the streets to tell the soldiers that Bella Sorrela for corned beef at Casa – no money, beautiful sister at house for no money but corned beef – fancy taking advantage of that! Girls weak with exhaustion had to be mauled for an hour or so for corned beef – that's life!

It was not uncommon for people to meet only in letters and fall in love never having seen each other. In 1940 seventeen-year-old Kathleen Healy had a tiff with her Welsh boyfriend and at a colleague's suggestion decided to write to a soldier in Gibraltar. She made a rough outline of how the letter would go, but found to her dismay that her colleague had helpfully posted it for her in its rough state. Undeterred, the soldier wrote back and they became pen-pals for three and a half years. Eventually they found an opportunity to meet at Stroud Station, overlooked by the Imperial Hotel:

You can visualise the dozens of heads leaning out of the hotel's windows to see what sort of soldier arrived to meet me.

The train came in, but no soldier got off. Just as Kathleen turned to leave, bitterly disappointed, the porter told her that the train

EXERCISE "BING ON!"   21st April, 1944.

QUESTIONS.	POINTS.

1. Where in Weymouth is there a CANNON BALL in the wall of a
   building, fired when the FRENCH attacked Weymouth. *The Old Tin Cabin*
2. What is the name of the Landlord (Licensee) of the SHIP INN at
   Preston....*Mr. S. ???*.....5.
3. What was the ROMAN NAME for DORCHESTER....*Durnovaria*.....5.
4. How many windows are there on the S. FRONT of the GLOUCESTER
   HOTEL Weymouth....*74*.....5.
5. Required One Copy of the DAILY HERALD of 17th April 1944....*S.S*....5.
6. What is the NAME of the OLDEST Railway Porter at the G.W.R. Station
   DORCHESTER (Westernmost Station)....*MR. FURSEY*.....8.
7. Who RIDES the WHITE HORSE OF OSMINGTON and which way is he
   heading....*King Geo. IIIrd. Faces from Weymouth East*.....8.
8. Required one Envelope bearing a W.R.N.S. Crest.....5.
9.   "   "   "   "   an A.T.S.   "   .....5.
10.   "   "   "   "   a W.A.A.F. "   .....5.
11. What was Queen Elizabeth's Straw Hat made of.....*STRAW*.....2.
12. What is the name of the INN at OSMINGTON MILLS....*??? Inn*....5.
13. How old is Mr. WINSTON CHURCHILL.....*69*.....2.
14. What is the Prime Minister's CHRISTIAN NAMES....*WINSTON SPENSER*.2.
15. How many CONCRETE BLOCKS are there in the sea wall from the last
    house of Melcombe Regis to the foot of FURZEY CLIFF....*456*....10.
16. What height is the highest point of MAIDEN CASTLE HILL near
    Winterborne Monkton......*400 ft*......8.
17. Required one ANISEED BALL.....10.
18. How many working levers are controlled by the SIGNALMAN at
    UPWEY JUNCTION STATION BOX.....10.
19. What is the name of the oldest member of the WEYMOUTH Lifeboat
    Crew - what is his duty in the crew....*Tom. ??? ???*.....8.
20. Required one Advert for ELIZABETHAN ARDEN COSMETICS....*GOT IT*...8.
22. What is the height above sea level of the LIGHT in the BILL
    OF PORTLAND LIGHTHOUSE....*300 ft*.....10.
23. Required one Horse Shoe....*GOT IT*.....6.
24. What is the name of the RIVER at DORCHESTER....*Frome*.....8.
25. What is the Number of the TELEPHONE at the CHALBURY LODGE ROAD
    JUNCTION BOX.....8.
26. How many MASTS are there in the WIRELESS STATION AT DORCHESTER....*17*...10.
27. What is the TELEPHONE number of the PUBLIC BOX at PRESTON POST
    OFFICE....*PRE. 2113*.....8.
28. What was the AMOUNT of the COLLECTION at Saint OSMUND'S CHURCH
    OSMINGTON on the 9th April....*??? ??? at ??? ??? next week* *Mr Mills collected*
29. How did WILLIAM FOOT die - buried in St. Osmund's Church Yard....*Short of breath*....
30. What colour is the SIGNAL at the SOUTHERN END of the RIDGEWAY
    TUNNEL on the UP Line from Weymouth to DORCHESTER....*??? 4 ft 6 in. Ridgeway ??? ??? Monmoth* *BLACK WHITE*
31. What is the above signal called in Railway Terms.....8.
32. Who is the BASKET MAKER of OSMINGTON VILLAGE....*Mr. Sharp*....12.
33. What NAME is on the TOWEL RAIL in the OUTSIDE GENTS LAVATORY at
    SUN RAY INN at OSMINGTON. *Pvt. Edw. ZABASZ KOWSKI*....10.
34. How many BIRDS are there in the Cage at the SUN RAY....*8*.....5.
35. What is the NAME of the LANDLORD (Licensee) at the BLACK DOG INN
    at BROADMAYNE....*SYDNEY COOPER*.....15.
36. From what BOOK of the BIBLE has the TEXT POSTED at the GATE of
    BROADMAYNE CHURCH been taken. *Rev. ch 3 v.17. Colossians 4 v.2*....15.
37. Approx how many YARDS is it round the OUTSIDE of the wall
    bounding the CHURCHYARD of WHITCOMBE CHURCH....*104 yds*.....20.
38. When was the MEMORIAL COFFEE TAVERN at DORCHESTER BUILT....*MDCCCLXXXI*....8.
39. What is the NAME of the LANDLORD of the NOAH'S ARK INN at DORCHESTER....8. *RIPPIN*
40. When was the OBELISK of the TOWN PUMP at DORCHESTER erected....*17.8.4*..10.
41. What was on the site of the TOWN PUMP at DORCHESTER before the OBELISK..8. *CUPOLA*
42. When was NAPIER'S ALMS HOUSE at DORCHESTER Built....*1616*.....10.
43. Who is the secretary of the HAND IN HAND LODGE of ODDFELLOWS at
    DORCHESTER....*H. MILLS*.....8.
44. Who gave the HORSE TROUGH outside the JUNCTION HOTEL
    at DORCHESTER and when did he give it....*G. HAMBRA. MP....1890*.8.
45. What is the WEEKLY ALLOWANCE for TOTAL DISABLEMENT by INJURY if you
    insure yourself with the Railway Passengers Assurance Company at 6d
    for return....*T.V. & Railway Co*.....10.
46. What evidence is there of COMBINED OPERATIONS TRAINING on the
    ROAD FROM DORCHESTER TO WEYMOUTH....*NONE*.....12.
47. When did WILLIAM VIRGIN the Elder die - buried in BINCOMBE CHURCH
    YARD, How old was he....*AGE 42. 9/1/1874*.....15.
48. Where is the VILLAGE BULL of BINCOMBE KEPT - in what DAIRY....25.
    No 1 BULL MOVED TO UPWEY YESTERDAY and 1 BULL LAST BOOK ON LEFT IN YARD AT BINCOMBE DAIRY

Royal Marine John Hampton filled in this light-hearted questionnaire on a day's shore exercise just before D-Day in 1944. The final question about a village bull led him to the farm where Land Army girl Gwendoline Notley was busy with the milking. This chance encounter led to a lasting romance.

was extra long and had pulled in twice. When her soldier alighted, they stared at each other: as agreed each was holding a photograph of the other. Overcome with embarrassment at being ogled by the hotel audience, Kathleen suggested that they both get back on to the train and go to her home in Cardiff. That evening, they walked up a hillside together. Her pen-friend suddenly stopped and said, 'Kathleen, I cannot go any further. Will you marry me?' She did and they were happy from that moment onwards.

During 1941 a group of office girls adopted a PoW through the British Red Cross. He was called George and was being kept in Camp 78 Sulmona in Italy. The girls took it in turns to write a few lines each in every letter. They sent him a photograph of themselves, each one identified by name and marital status. He kept that photograph with him at all times, but the girls lost touch with him when he was moved to Austria. He was repatriated in 1945 via the Russians and the Americans.

After the war he wrote to say he was back home and could he meet the girls and thank them personally for all their newsy letters and parcels. A party was arranged with some male office workers as well so that George shouldn't feel ill at ease and embarrassed by so many women. It was a happy occasion, but George was only thinking about one girl, Mary, identified in the photograph as 'brunette, single'. Two days later he invited her out on her own and their friendship turned to love and a 'superbly happy marriage'. Mary wrote:

The astounding thing is, when George Sevenoaks first received the photograph from the office, he told the other PoWs in the hut they shared that I was the young lady he would be most interested in.

John Hampton, a corporal in the Royal Marines, was serving on a landing craft in Portland Harbour, awaiting D-Day. Shore leave was very hard to come by and the sailors grabbed at any excuse to get off the ship. When volunteers were called for to take part in a day's exercise ashore he and many others from the flotilla jumped at the chance. It turned out to be a long day's trek around Weymouth and the Dorchester area, gathering all kinds of information on a questionnaire form entitled 'Exercise "Bang On", 21 April 1944'. The questions were in a light-hearted quiz form: What is the name of the landlord of the Ship Inn at Preston? How many yards round

Brought together in 1944 by an obscure question about a village bull, Sergeant John Hampton DSM of the Royal Marines and Land Army girl Gwendoline Notley were married at the end of the war. She wore a dress made from material sent by John from India where he had been serving after taking part in the D-Day landings. The photograph of Gwendoline with the bull is a reminder of the unusual origins of their meeting.

the churchyard wall at Whitcombe? What name is on the towel rail in the outside gents lavatory at the Sun Ray Inn at Osmington? and so on. They walked and hitchhiked, and scrounged lunch at a US army camp at Friar Mayne.

On the return journey from Dorchester my oppo and I were trying to establish the whereabouts of the Bincombe Bull (Question No 48). After trying 2 farms in the area with little help from the locals we decided to give up, but going up the hill on the way to Broadway we passed a corrugated

This note was tucked into the packaging of a map-pocket by a girl working in an aircraft factory during the Second World War. Perhaps she dreamed that it might be found by a dashing pilot who would whisk her away from the monotony of her daily life?

iron cow stall and decided on one more try, so in we went. There we found the dairyman and his wife (Mr and Mrs Riggs) milking about 30 cows by hand and quietly milking away on a three-legged stool was a very pretty and very shy Land Army girl named Gwendoline. Now what could a Royal do? But try milking a cow (Hopeless!!) and also trying very hard to make a date, which I eventually did for the following evening; but this was only after my oppo was cross questioned if my intentions were honourable and a satisfactory reply obtained.

Now my real troubles were only just beginning. How to get ashore again to keep this date? Fortunately I had a gem of an Officer Lt (Pony) Moore RM who when I told him my story twisted all the rules and broke others to make it possible for me to get ashore for this special date and 2 or 3 more afterwards before the off.

Gwendoline (this Land Army girl) lived in Upwey, which is only about 3 miles as the crow flies from Weymouth Bay and Portland Harbour. These can both be seen from parts of Upwey. She knew we must have sailed because they were awakened early on the 6th to the sound of planes and gliders going over and the heavy traffic movements through the village.

After the landing in Normandy, John Hampton was posted to India

and Burma and finally to Singapore – he and Gwendoline became engaged while he was in India, but they didn't meet again until 1946, when they were married on his demob leave in April. The question about the location of the Bincombe Village Bull, besides being the last on the questionnaire, had carried the most points. To John it turned out to be more valuable than he could ever have guessed.

When Brian May and Frank Hall were restoring a de Havilland Tiger Moth recently, they used parts from a multitude of sources. Tiger Moths were used during the Second World War to train pilots all over the world, and May and Hall were labouring with painstaking care to make sure every detail was accurate and authentic. Some components were still in their original packaging which protected them after manufacture.

When Claire Potter responded to the appeal to send Christmas gifts to soldiers in the Gulf in 1990, she had no idea that she would eventually marry the soldier who received her card.

Tucked away in a map-pocket which was still in the manufacturer's packaging the two men came across a little pencil-written note. It said:

Alice Day, Thomlinson Avenue, Raffles, Carlisle. Dark and good looking.

Claire Abbott chose a Christmas card with a snow scene on it, a typically English village with a beamed house and a church. Inside she wrote:

Hi – we are all thinking of you lads back home, hope your Xmas won't be too bad. If any one wants a pen-pal I am eighteen and a half with no ties, I am a Care Nurse and also work a few nights in a night club.

Then she added her name and address and put it into an envelope, on which she wrote, 'To a soldier, c/o 7th Armoured Brigade, BFPO 644'. She posted it in a parcel of Christmas presents for soldiers serving in the desert on 14 December 1990. Nine days later, Lance Corporal Potter wrote back:

Hello there! My name is Dougie and I happen to be the lucky chap who received the Christmas card you sent to a soldier in the Gulf. May I begin by saying Thank you, it was really very kind of you to spare a thought for us out here.

Dougie was a prolific writer. Claire sent him parcels and letters and photographs and Dougie's enthusiastic responses were all the proof Claire needed to know that the small effort to boost morale was having a profound effect. They met on leave in March 1991 and were married on 16 December, a year to the day after he received her first letter.

The little pink flower that Lou Tibbert carried with him all through the war. He had met Jessie at a dance at Lichfield Barracks and took the velvet flower from her dance dress as a keepsake before he left with the North Staffordshire Regiment to be posted abroad. They married in 1941.

OPPOSITE: The sudden departure of British forces to the Gulf after the invasion of Kuwait in 1990 reawakened in many servicemen and their sweethearts the forgotten art of letter-writing. Royal Mail International 'blueys' were filled with the fears, longings and hopes of those in the front line, and those waiting anxiously at home.

— 3 —
LETTERS

'While you're away, O please remember me'

All being well, I'll come to you
Sweetheart, before the year is through;
And we shall find so much to do,
So much to tell.

I read your letter through and through,
And dreamt of all we'd say and do
Till in my heart the thought of you
Rang like a bell.

Wilfred Gibson – *All Being Well*

A soldier serving with the Desert Rats in the Gulf in February 1991 puts his thoughts into words before his unit moves in for the main offensive.

During periods of separation letters were the mainstay of loving relationships. They not only carried news and expressions of love, but were an opportunity to dream, particularly for the serviceman far from the comfort and routine of home life. Sometimes it was easier to write what you felt rather than say it. To the recipient, the letters were physical representations of the writer, the handwriting speaking as clearly as a voice, the fact that beloved hands had actually touched that piece of paper bringing an almost magical quality to letter and envelope. They could be carried in battledress pockets close to the heart, tied with ribbons, kept in boxes and re-read in moments of loneliness.

People found that they were freed by writing and embarked on poems and drawings and expressions couched in terms they might not have thought of in peacetime. Time and again, home is what is longed for, normal daily things, walking hand in hand, sitting by rivers or strolling through fields, being with the one true love in a peaceful world. The dreams never seemed to include great wealth or power or travel, or any kind of glamour. From the men at war there was very little carping about conditions; even after long descriptions of discomfort or misery there is a cheerful exhortation to 'keep smiling' or 'not to worry'. By writing optimistically the serviceman kept his own spirits up; in a way he may have been addressing himself, too.

However, both those who were away and those who stayed at home were facing worlds which were quite new. For the women, there was the struggle of running a home and looking after children through times of rationing and deprivation, anxiety, boredom and even temptation; trying to make do on tiny amounts of money, managing to keep the idea of 'Daddy' alive in the minds of tiny children who had nearly forgotten him or perhaps had never known him at all. For the man, often away from home for the first time in his life, there was the excitement and homesickness that travel can bring, fear, boredom and the powerlessness of being a pawn moved about by higher authorities and not knowing where he was going or for how long. There were anxieties about his sweetheart's faithfulness, coupled with his own needs and desires, and the knowledge that he was living through experiences he could never share with the one he loved. But despite these pressures, letters often cemented love affairs together and even from the

Irrepressibly good-humoured, even in the mud and squalor of the trenches, Alfred Bland wrote frequently to his wife until his death on the first day of the Battle of the Somme on 1 July 1916.

darkest corners of wartime brought hope and the determination to grin and bear it.

After two months in France in 1916, in the most depressing, soaking mud-bath with death all around him, Captain Alfred Bland, serving with a battalion of the Manchester Regiment, wrote this, one of many extraordinarily endearing letters to his wife Violet. Six months later he was killed at the Battle of the Somme.

My only and eternal blessedness,

I wonder whether you resent my cheerfulness ever! Do you, dear? Because you might, you know. I ought, by the rules of love, to spend my days and nights in an eternity of sighs and sorrow for our enforced parting. And by all the rules of war, I ought to be enduring cold and hardship, hunger and fatigue, bitterness of soul and dismay of heart. Alas! What shall I say in my defence? Because not even Merriman can depress me, and as for the CO I am simply impertinent to him, while the dull routine of being behind the line fills me with an inexhaustible supply of cheerful patience. What shall we say about it? Would it rejoice you if I confessed to being utterly miserable every now and then? If I told you how I loathed war and hated every minute that prolonged it? If I admitted that I yearn hourly for my return, my final return away from it all? If I said that I hated my brother officers and was sick of the sight of the Company? If I described the filthy squalor of the village streets, the sickening repetition of low clouds and sulky drizzle and heavy rain, and the dreary monotony of ration beef and ration bread. Would you be glad or sorry? Oh, I *know* how sympathetic and sad you would feel, and I *know* you would *not* be glad at all. Would you? And if you *were* glad, you would be all wrong; because, even if these things were true, it wouldn't bring us together again, it wouldn't make me love you more, it wouldn't sweeten those embraces we are deprived of for the

Captain Fred Hardman kept this photograph of his wife and son beside him when he wrote to them from the trenches.

moment, it wouldn't strengthen our divine oneness one scrap. Would it?
No, my darling, thank the heavens daily that in all circumstances you will
be right in picturing your boy out here simply brimming over with gaiety
irrepressible. I am becoming a byword. Cushion says, 'I *like* you, Bill Bland.'
Why? Because I am always laughing with everybody and everything,
greeting the seen and the unseen with a cheer. And it isn't a pose. It's the
solemn truth. So let us go back again to those imaginary admissions above.
I am *never* utterly miserable, not even when I yearn most for the touch of
your lips and a sight of my boys. Why? Because I am in France, where the
war is, and I know I ought to be here. And I don't loathe war, I love 95%
of it, and hate the thought of it being ended too soon. And I don't yearn
hourly for my final return, although I am very pleasantly excited at the
possibility of 9 days leave in March, which indeed we haven't earned by
any means so far. And I don't loathe my brother officers but love them
more than I dreamed possible, and as for my Company, why bless it! And
the mud is such *friendly* mud, somehow, so yielding and considerate – and
I don't have to clean my own boots. And I have lost the habit of regarding
the weather, for if it rains, we get wet, and if it doesn't, we don't, and if
the sun shines, how nice! And as for our food, well, I've given you an idea
of *that* before, and I have nothing to add to the statements made in this
House on November 30 and December 6 last or any other time. No, dear,
whether you like it or not, I *am* fundamentally happy and on the surface
childishly gay. And there's an end on't.

Post just going. Good night, darling.

Ever your
Alfred.

No matter how grim the surroundings or hopeless the conditions,
letters from the front were often full of this optimism and
philosophical good humour. Captain Fred Hardman was serving
with his regiment, the 10th Manchesters, in Northern France
during the First World War when he wrote this letter home,
enclosing roses for his wife.

My dear Kit,

There is something beautiful even on the battlefields of France, and
these roses I have plucked for you, which were struggling to live among
the nettles and thorns of this desolated village.

As they have lived, so you must live and lift up your heart when the
world is lonely and sad, and after all, there is something beautiful in this
troubled universe of ours. My fond love I send to you and our boys.

Your Devoted Hubby,
Fred.

Douglas Talbot was still at school, cramming for Sandhurst, when he first met Mary Turle and her younger sister, Dorothy. Their uncle was his tutor, and friendship soon developed between Douglas and the girls; he became extremely close particularly to Dorothy, or 'Dorfie' as he called her, although their ten-year relationship was platonic, 'an affair of the intellect and the heart, not of the body'. Douglas and Dorfie shared a love of nature, of walking and of poetry, and when serving as a captain at Gallipoli, he wrote vivid, lively letters to Dorfie which she kept until she died, aged eighty-seven. Captain Douglas Talbot was killed at Gallipoli; although Dorothy later married his closest friend, Major Tom Slingsby, and lived happily with him for sixty years, Douglas was the great love of her life. These extracts from two of his letters show the depth of his feelings for her.

Oh! You simply have been haunting me lately. I have really been able to picture you. I suppose it is these times our souls yearn more than ever for communion. I see you now in your dear grey dress, now in the town kit, with the fur round your neck, leaning against the mantel at Inverness Terrace and saying, 'I want to be kissed by you!' What a fool I was. You would not have to wait long now. No. Don't blush. No one shall read this letter as I shall censor it myself. You bear witness that what I have said will not help the Turks.

Dorfie, when will, and what will, be the end of all this? Life is desperately hard, you are right. How many people have lived and loved in such hard times as these now present? Somehow the war is bearing me up. That go of malaria took all my bodily and mental strength away – if it had not been for your existence I should have longed to die. Now I know how sweet life can be. I have seen death all round me and although it is very beautiful and the more you see the more you believe in the future, I simply long for the day when the cloud shall lift and we shall be together again in peace.

. . . How much would I give for a shady lawn, a comfy chair and you in a hammock beside me; free as a bird in the air; at times this war seems to be going to be more than I can bear, but I know I really can bear much more, knowing what I have behind me, our love. I picture you in the grey army kit, walking along with your hands behind your back; I have often done so before. When I had fever at Karachi, I think I told you there was a nurse there who reminded me very much of you, at least she seemed to be like you to my fevered brain; and the touch of her cool hand on my brow was yours entirely, so don't be jealous.

Oh yes, Dorfie girl, won't it be topping to sit on a cool shady bank and

watch the trout etc. Somehow I feel the sights I have seen in this war will make me a hundred times more humane in my sport; and yet sport does help you to understand war, as you say, but our love helps more than all these days.

 God bless you girl,
  Your Douglas boy.

   Wife Longing

   Saturday evening –
   Alone –
   Reading her letter,
   The beloved hand has written
   'Can come on Friday.'
   Friday!
   Six days of longing,
   Pain, excitement.
   Six days of lying a-bed
   In agony
   Of possession-anticipation.

   The station-meeting
   How will it happen?
   I know so well –
   So well.

   Breathless station-wards rush –
   Train late
   (Why is that wife-bringing train is ever
   Late – wife-taking train is ever prompt?)

   Three – five – six cigarettes
   And with nerve-destroying cacophony
   The platform is filled
   With train.
   Scores – hundreds of nondescripts
   Will swarm
   Past the anxiously-watching
   Myopic
   Subaltern.

   Then –
   Suddenly –

Their colours still glowing brightly after seventy-five years, these beautiful hand-embroidered cards were sent home from France by British soldiers to their wives and girlfriends.

PAM
PAM
PAM.
Fur hat – glasses –
Snuggly coat – green case –
Brown eyes – glorious mouth,
Peach-bloom face –
Tiny ears – perfect teeth.
PAM – MY WIFE,
MY WIFE – PAM.
(How do you do!)

Station-porter
Sees gauche man and
Dainty woman
Exchange
Husband-wife-wife-husband-kiss.
But
Sees not
The warm,
Soft,
Desire-creating
Tongues.
Body-electrifying thrill
At
Lover's contact.
Nor accelerating heart beats.

Tram ride
Bus ride
Joyous talk
Short walk.
MRS LANDLADY – MY WIFE,
MY WIFE – MRS LANDLADY.
(How do you do!)

Bed-room (wife-photo-littered) –
Outstretched arms –
'Come on, Pam!'
Welded lips
And bodies.
Mutual possession –
Desire appeased

Cara lettera...

This postcard, sent to an Italian soldier by his girlfriend, Lucia, was picked up on a North African battlefield by a British airman in November 1942. The image and message are universal, regardless of the language or the side on which the soldier is fighting.

But
Not satiated.

Pain, craving and self-possession
Of forty-one days' parting
Forgotten,
Everything
Forgotten
Except dazzling, sacred, ecstatic realisation
Of loved one's presence
And love.

To earth again,
Six days.
Six days?
YEARS.
Years of longing, pain,
Excitement and
Possession-anticipation.

Longing, pain,
Excitement and
Possession-anticipation.

Lieutenant M.G. Odell
819 SMOKE COY PC
LUTON.
December 1943.

A pouch containing a miniature of his wife and a shoe worn by his baby son, kept by a soldier in a pocket next to his heart throughout the time he was in the trenches. Almost every serviceman carried with him some physical reminder of his loved ones.

The summer of 1940 was long and hot. Only ten days after she had left school aged seventeen and a half, Julia Lee-Booker met Major Pat McSwiney and they fell in love. Pat proposed to her a fortnight later, but they agreed for her family's sake to wait until she was older before they married. They were separated for over three years during which time they wrote constantly to each other. These extracts are from some of Julia's letters; as a footnote written fifty years later she remembers:

People were happy in a funny sort of way. You adapted to each day as it came and you seldom made plans for the future. You didn't need to make choices and we were all in it together. The camaraderie amongst people living in each other's pockets and sharing a common purpose defies description.

The first of her letters recalls the blissful feeling of being young and in love:

July 24th, 1940.

I cannot get that beautiful afternoon out of my head, above me where I lay the grass was silhouetted against the blue of the heavens, small clouds were rushing past as the wind drove them on an endless journey. Then close to me was the most lovely of all, your soft hair against my cheek, your kisses so cool and unearthly and my happiness was so great. Yesterday I revisited our walks round the cliffs at Perran, the spot where you first kissed me looking down on that derelict mine shaft, it brings back sweet memories indeed. Your beautiful crucifix is a constant reminder of you, my sweetheart.

July (cont).

Mummy says tell Pat the Truro and Perranporth Home Guard are held up from their duties through lack of trousers! They've got their Gor Blimey caps and coats but *no* trousers.

I'm quite seriously thinking of joining the ATS when I'm 18 and Mummy and Daddy want to know what you think about it? In due course all girls will be mobilised and so it would be better to join up before it becomes compulsory. The work is varied and not boring.

Hugh Sinclair (a film star) said about us, 'You look so marvellous together, I do hope you marry Pat!'

Over an hour has elapsed since I wrote those last words, the sirens had gone and the noise of the 'planes and bombs distracted me too much. Now the 'All Clear' is through, but the searchlights are over Falmouth and scattered crumps are still in progress.

February 27th, 1942.

Well, surprise, here I am aged 19, the youngest Petty Officer of ten on a station of now 400 Wrens. There has been controversy as I was considered too young at 19, most are over 26. I think my tricorn hat is flattering, I have brass buttons and can be out until any hour! I now earn nearly £2 a week and weigh 9 stone 7! A sea mist is blowing so I am drenched. Last night's dance broke up in the middle of a raid and we had to sit in the air-raid shelter singing songs.

July 1943.

I've had three airgraphs from you, lovely. I have had a wonderful afternoon off-duty – three pilots took me out to tea. We went down to the beach, ate masses and did handstands and somersaults! Sandwiches and drinks at the Trevose Golf Club and down to the beach again. We

didn't get back until nearly midnight. I wasn't on duty until midday today, lucky for me as I overslept! I'm sure I feel very shy meeting your parents and your parents' friend. Mrs Tuite-Dalton thought I was quiet – she doesn't really know me! Thank you so much for all your lovely letters.

October 31st, 1943.

P my dearest one, I shall never be good enough for you, but please remember how I adore you. If our love can last three years without seeing one another, it will last for ever if we take great care of it.

Jan 5th, 1944.

I dream about you frequently, my darling, and we just stand and hug one another. I must be one of the few Wrens who hasn't been out with an American.

January 19th, 1944.

Your letter came with the hopeful news of your coming back to go to the Staff College. I am due for leave and might get six weeks unpaid leave to get married and live with you in digs in Camberley. Pat darling, I do believe our patience has at last been rewarded.

Julia and Pat started their long and happy married life soon afterwards.

Writing constantly to each other, couples sometimes expressed a fear that their letters were repetitive or that they had said 'I love you' too often. Sergeant Tommy Kilfoyle writing from the Sergeants' Mess at RAF Stradishall, near Newmarket, implores his wife to carry on saying those three precious words:

Hello Precious,

I have been reading through your letters again. I am most annoyed. Take off your hat, you're on a charge. ME: 'How dare you have the temerity to suggest that I might get bored with the number of times you say you love me?' YOU: 'Well I – er – er, thought – er . . .' ME: 'Stop stammering, woman. I am going to punish you for careless talk. I hereby sentence you to 14 days on Form Serial No 295, so long as you spend it with your

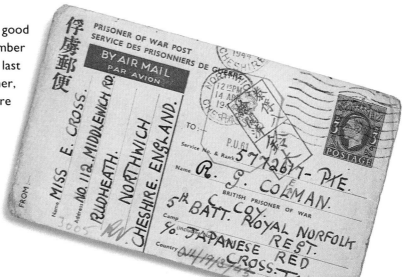

Prisoners of war in the Far East received the barest quantity of mail from home. This card was sent in April 1944 by Evelyn Cross to Private Ronald Coleman, a prisoner in a Japanese PoW camp. It took eleven months to arrive . . .

... **Communication with Far Eastern PoWs was limited to officially-issued postcards on which just twenty-five words were permitted. One can only wonder at the strength of spirit of many couples whose relationships survived in these circumstances.**

husband. Next charge please!'

Non! Mais non! Mon cheri, I shall never tire of hearing you say those words. I adore you above everything in this world completely and unceasingly and no one can say more about their loves. I tell you, darling, regarding you, I can out-Romeo Romeo himself. So –! So –! Why should I get bored when you tell me those three words, that mean more than life itself to me? Don't you understand if you were not here to say those words, or by some terrible stroke of fate, you ceased to love me, life would not mean anything any more? Keep on telling me, darling, don't ever stop, and don't even think I'll get bored by hearing them.

... Darling, yesterday during that last 15 minutes on the station, I felt really bucked. Life did seem to take on a really roseate hue, and it bucked me up no end to see you smile, the way you did. You are really wonderful, darling, and you do have such a marvellous effect on me

Darling, Bad News – No B——Y PAY until next week. What a to do. Still as soon as it arrives I shall send some on to you, so keeping hoping. Well, Darling, in two or three minutes time I have a date to keep with the most sweet and loveliest darling wife in the world. You see at 10.30 I have a date with you, and as it is only now a couple of minutes off I will finish this letter and talk to you for a little time.

Goodnight, Darling, and God Bless You, and keep you safe for me, always.

I love you
Loads and Loads and Loads
Ever and Ever. Ad infinitum.
   Your loving husband,
   Tommy.

OPPOSITE: **A booklet prepared by Charles Warrell called** *I'll Teach You Better Letter-Writing* **was on sale for ninepence. The difficulties of writing the same thing frequently were addressed by Mr Warrell; a separate section deals with the particular problems of keeping home news lively and optimistic in a letter to a serviceman far away.**

Peter Merrill, between bombing raids, kept a detailed diary account of the day's events especially for his girlfriend, later to become his wife. He wrote letters as well, but in his diary he was able to combine technical jargon with heartfelt longings as though he were thinking out loud: the diary is a refuge at the end of a day of exhilaration and terror.

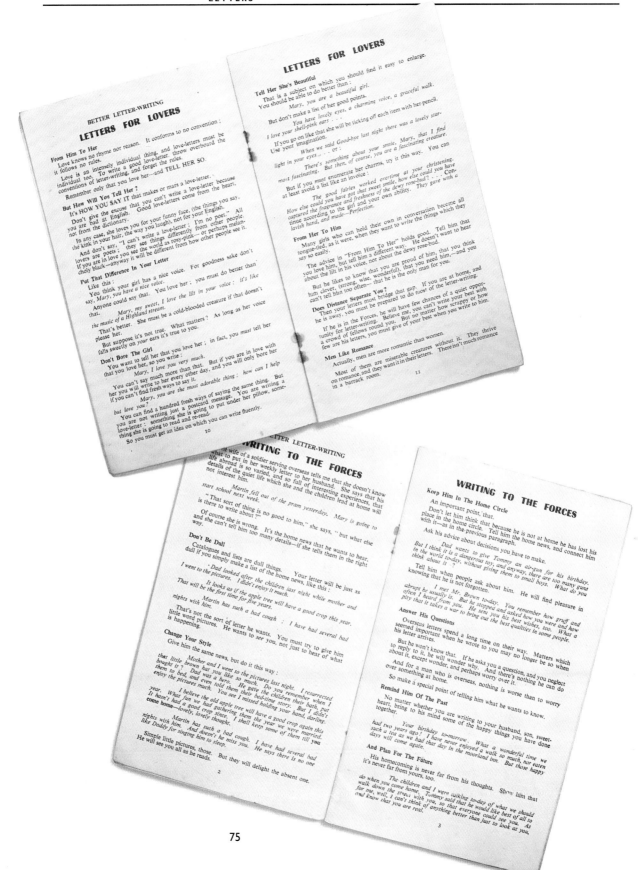

BETTER LETTER-WRITING
LETTERS FOR LOVERS

From Him To Her

Love knows no rhyme nor reason. It conforms to no convention; it follows no rules.

Love is an intensely individual thing, and love-letters must be individual too. To write a good love-letter, throw overboard the conventions of letter-writing, and forget the rules.

Remember only that you love her—and TELL HER SO.

But How Will You Tell Her?

It's HOW YOU SAY IT that makes or mars a love-letter.

Don't give the excuse that you can't write a love-letter because you are bad at English. Good love-letters come from the heart, not from the dictionary.

In any case, she loves you for your funny face, (the things you say, the kink in your hair, the way you laugh), not for your English." All lovers are poets; "I can't write a love-letter: I'm no poet." And don't say, "they see things differently from other people. If you are in love you see the world as rosy-pink—or perhaps melancholy black—anyway it will be different from how other people see it.

Put That Difference In Your Letter

Like this:

You think your girl has a nice voice. For goodness sake don't say, *Mary, you have a nice voice.*

Anyone could say that. You love her; you must do better than that.

Mary, my sweet, I love the lilt in your voice: it's like the music of a Highland stream.

That's better. She must be a cold-blooded creature if that doesn't please her.

But suppose it's not true. What matters? As long as her voice falls sweetly on your ears it's true to you.

Don't Bore The Girl

You want to tell her that you love her; in fact, you *must* tell her that you love her, so you write :

Mary, I love you very much.

You can't say much more than that. But if you are in love with her you will write to her every other day, and you will only bore her if you can't find fresh ways to say it.

Mary, you are the most adorable thing : how can I help but love you?

You can find a hundred fresh ways of saying the same thing. You are writing a love-letter; something she is going to put under her pillow, something she is going to read and re-read.

So you must get an idea on which you can write fluently.

10

LETTERS FOR LOVERS

Tell Her She's Beautiful

That is a subject on which you should find it easy to enlarge. You should be able to do better than :

Mary, you are a beautiful girl.

But don't make a list of her good points.

You have lovely eyes, a charming voice, a graceful walk. I love your shell-pink ears . . .

If you go on like that she will be ticking off each item with her pencil. Use your imagination.

When we said Good-bye last night there was a lovely star-light in your eyes . . . or :

There's something about your smile, Mary, that I find most fascinating. But then, of course, you are a fascinating creature.

But if you must enumerate her charms, try it this way. Con-tinue according to the girl and your own ability. They gave with a lavish hand, and made—Perfection.

From Her To Him

Many girls who can hold their own in conversation become all tongue-tied, as it were, when they want to write the things which they say so easily.

The advice in "From Him To Her" holds good. Tell him that you love him, but tell him a different way. He doesn't want to hear about the lilt in his voice, nor about the dewy rose-bud.

But he likes to know that you are proud of him, that you think him clever, (strong, wise, wonderful), that you need him.—and you can't tell him too often—that he is the only man for you.

Does Distance Separate You?

Then your letters must bridge that gap. If you are at home, and he is away, you must be prepared to use most of the letter-writing.

If he is in the Forces, he will have few chances of a quiet oppor-tunity for letter-writing. Believe me, you can't write your best with a crowd of fellows round you. But no matter how scrappy or how few are his letters, you must give of your best when you write to him.

Men Like Romance

Actually, men are more romantic than women. They thrive on romance, and they want it in their letters. There isn't much romance in a barrack room.

11

BETTER LETTER-WRITING
WRITING TO THE FORCES

The wife of a soldier serving overseas tells me that she doesn't know what to put in her weekly letter to her husband. She says that his life abroad is so varied, and so full of interesting experiences, that details of the quiet life which she and the children lead at home will not interest him.

Martin fell out of the pram yesterday. Mary is going to start school next week.

"That sort of thing is no good to him," she says, "but what else is there to write about?"

Of course she is wrong. It's the home news that he wants to hear, and she can't tell him too many details—if she tells them in the right way.

Don't Be Dull

Catalogues and lists are dull things. Your letter will be just as dull if you simply make a list of the home news, like this :

I went to the pictures last night.
Dad looked after the children last night while mother and I went to the pictures. I didn't enjoy it much.

It looks as if the apple tree will have a good crop this year.
That will be the first time for five years.

Martin has such a bad cough : I have had several bad nights with him.

That's not the sort of letter he wants. You must try to give him little word pictures. He wants to see you, not just to hear of what is happening.

Change Your Style

Give him the same news, but do it this way :

Mother and I went to the pictures last night. I resurrected that little brown hat you like so much. Dad was a hero. I bought it . . . Do you remember when I bought it ? Dad was a hero. He gave the children their bath, put them to bed, and even told them their bed-time story. But I didn't enjoy the pictures much. You see I missed holding your hand, darling.

year. I believe the old apple tree will have a good crop again this It hasn't had a good crop since. What fun we had gathering them the year we were married. come home—lovely, lovely thought. I shall keep some of them till you

Martin has such a bad cough. He miss you. nights with him, like Daddy for singing him to sleep. I have had several bad

Simple little pictures, those. He will see you all as he reads. But they will delight the absent one.

2

WRITING TO THE FORCES

Keep Him In The Home Circle

An important point, that.

Don't let him think that because he is not at home he has lost his place in the home circle. Tell him the home news, and connect him with it—as in the previous paragraph.

Ask his advice about decisions you have to make.

Dad wants to give Tommy an air-gun for his birthday. But I think it is a dangerous toy, and anyway, there are too many guns in the world to-day, without giving them to small boys. What do you think about it ?

Tell him when people ask about him. He will find pleasure in knowing that he is not forgotten.

I met Mr. Brown to-day. You remember how gruff and abrupt he usually is. But he stopped and asked how you were and how often I heard from you. He sent you his best wishes, too. What a pity that it takes a war to bring out the best qualities in some people.

Answer His Questions

Overseas letters spend a long time on their way. Matters which seemed important when he wrote to you may no longer be so when his letter arrives.

But he won't know that. If he asks you a question, and you neglect to reply to it, he will wonder why. And there's nothing he can do about it, except wonder, and perhaps worry over it.

And for a man who is overseas, nothing is worse than to worry over something at home.

So make a special point of telling him what he wants to know.

Remind Him Of The Past

No matter whether you are writing to your husband, son, sweet-heart, bring to his mind some of the happy things you have done together.

Your birthday to-morrow. What a wonderful time we had two years ago ! I have never enjoyed a walk so much, nor eaten such a tea as we had that day in the moorland inn. But those happy days will come again.

And Plan For The Future

His homecoming is never far from his thoughts. Show him that it's never far from yours, too.

The children and I were walking to-day of what we should do when you come home, Tommy said that he would like best of all to walk down the street with you, so that everyone could see you. As for me, well, I can't think of anything better than just to look at you, and know that you are real.

3

Friday October 20th 1944.

Got up 8.10. Made a switch for the light, but then found that the bulb was broken. Went down to the plane after dinner for DI as we are flying tonight. Briefed at 3 p.m. Target a night-fighter drome at Szombathely, Hungary. Started to write a letter to Margaret but had to leave it as we took off at 6.40 p.m. The Skipper's mike went for a Burton so he borrowed mine. Didn't see much on the way out, a little Flak. Got to the target just as the flares were going down. The Markers were late, so Tom bombed visually. Only one bomb went, so he salvoed the rest. Saw a few fighters taking off, and was chased by one for about ten minutes on the way back, but managed to avoid him by corkscrewing. Had to alter course to get out of 6 searchlights and didn't see much else.

Was just coming in to land when Dan said the nose wheel was still retracted and he couldn't get it out, so I had to go and undo the catch and after a lot of struggling managed to throw it out. It nearly took me with it, but the slipstream blew me back in again.

I was thinking of you a lot tonight and was wondering if I should ever see you again, but strange to say I didn't feel a bit scared. I love you so much, sweetheart, and know God will grant me a safe conduct back to you. Pleasant dreams, dearest.

Parted when their little daughter was only a few months old, Gerald and Mavis Bunyan had no need of Charles Warrell's booklet to keep their correspondence vivid and informative. Gerald was posted with the RAF to India and the Far East. They numbered their letters to each other as mail sometimes took several weeks to reach its destination and questions and answers could become unsynchronised.

No. 13. Mauripur, 17 December '43.
My beloved,

How are you and Lesley Ann keeping? I'm trusting lots and lots that you are quite OK, because I haven't heard from you yet. Just keep on writing all the time and I shall suddenly have a load of mail. I hope my mail is reaching you quickly 'cos it will save a lot of complications in addresses later on. Every minute is so horrible without you, my darling, and I am longing to see you and be with you again for always. I don't know how long I will be at this address but I'll try to let you know in good time. Letters will be OK but don't be tempted to send parcels or anything like that until I send you a more or less permanent address. It will be wonderful to hear what you have been doing, and all Lesley Ann's tricks. Years seem to have passed since our holiday at Blackpool but even in that comparatively short

OPPOSITE: **Mavis Bunyan and her husband Gerald, serving with the RAF, were separated for two and a half long years during the Second World War. During that time they exchanged 1,259 letters. Their daughter, Lesley Ann, was only nine months old when Gerald left, and Mavis tried to give him 'word pictures' of her so he could share the first years of her young life.**

Birthday and Valentine cards sent by Gerald Bunyan to his wife Mavis.

time she must have given you lots of fun. I'm 'glad as glad' that Lesley Ann 'happened' 'cos I know that you are being taken care of. I wish I could have just one peep at you two, you probably back at the office, and Lesley Ann in a day nursery or worrying your mum to death! Since I last wrote to you I've been travelling about – as you can see from the address we are now in the desert. This is desert but fairly civilised desert! We are billeted very comfortably and have a decent clean mess – totally different from the filthy conditions during the train journey! I won't tell you about it in this letter 'cos I started another 'history' airmail letter this morning. I know you think I'm a rogue but I haven't been able to have a solo photograph taken yet, but I won't forget my promise. One of the lads took a snap of six of us and I'll let you have one when they are developed. He cannot take a 'solo' because of the terrible shortage of films. There are quite a number of camels round here and it is amusing to see them plodding about the place, harnessed to rubber-tyred carts! It reminds me of 'East is East . . . etc.', but works very well. Every morning we are wakened by the tinkling of camel bells and a morning cup of tea brought in by a bearer. I'm not pulling your leg – even though it is very nice! Last night three of us went to a YMCA on the camp and listened to a gramophone concert. Emperor Concerto and Unfinished Symphony were the highlights. The bottom of the page is very near now so cheerio, my always beloved girl, and God bless you.

I love you every minute for always,
Your Gerald.

PS I love you and kiss Lesley Ann for me.

At the time of writing this next letter, Mavis has received a huge bouquet of flowers from Gerald on her twentieth birthday. She has taken a job as a bus conductress, and tells her husband of meeting a lonely American pilot who travels on her bus.

No 183. 4.7.44.
My precious boy,

In front of me as I write are such lots of lovely flowers. Although I love them, darling, I love your message more, though. I do love you beyond all imagining, my sweetheart, and I want you beyond all expression. My love for you is so terrible, because in this parting it brings such desolation and heartache. Now I must tell you about my birthday, and it has been one of surprises. This morning an American flyer rode up and down on my bus. We discovered much in common. He has a little boy 15 months old, and his wife is ten months younger than me. When I mentioned it was my birthday he asked if he could take me to dinner. He was wounded in the

stomach by flak over France and is recuperating here at one of the hotels that have been taken over. Not wanting a repetition of the desolation of last night at being parted on our anniversary, I said yes and asked him to tea so that he could see Lesley Ann and maybe get an idea of how his own baby is now 'cos he was three weeks old when he last saw him. He came and brought me six gorgeous carnations. After tea I was just getting ready to go out when Clarence came. He was filthy and had just got back from France, the only one of his group left. He is staying the night and tomorrow is going on to his station which is quite near here. He is hoping to get some leave. When he walked in, beloved, my heart ached until I could hardly bear it. I wanted to cry because it was not you. I imagined how wonderful it would be if only I could have rushed into your arms if it was you and not just him. What a wonderful night we should have spent together, just you and I. Instead of that it was a handshake with Clarence. I do love you so much, nothing eases this horrible ache and need of you. Goodnight, my beloved. I hope you will be here for my next birthday. Please God that you will.

    Ever your own, Mavis.

Vernon Browne, a photographer with the 21st Army Group in Germany, took this pensive picture of a soldier composing a letter home surrounded by the debris of war.

79

No 408. 92 Mobile FC Unit 13.7.45.

My beloved girl,

It is nearly bedtime but I just couldn't turn in without saying 'I love you'. I have just come back from a mobile cinema show – the film was *Bathing Beauty*. It is strange – or maybe not so strange – but the beauty of the colours made me think so much of you. The many 'luscious' girls had no effect on me except to increase my longing for you almost to breaking point. I love you until the wanting and desire of you, the ache in my heart, and the loneliness threaten to engulf me completely.

Even in spite of the men around me, that loneliness is always there 'cos only you matter. I long so terribly to crush you into my arms and feel your body pressing closer and closer with each breath. Oh darling, I will go nuts if I don't see you soon 'cos the desire is nearly bursting me. I want to kiss your soft loveliness and feel your warm lips on mine as our bodies become as one. Tonight there will be no you to caress, no dear breasts uplifting to my kisses, no scent of your hair – in fact, nothing at all. Your heart will be with me but my sleep will be empty, so different from the glorious contentment of having you beside me all the time. Please, I want so badly to be your real husband again and not just a bloke away from home whose heart is breaking to be with you.

Today, my lovely, there was no mail from you and I was so disappointed. It is greedy of me really 'cos they come through quickly. Letters! Letters! Letters! They are all we have and they should be kisses – sweetly intimate kisses arising from our physical love. I seem tongue-tied and cannot find words enough to mirror the thoughts of my heart. If we were together, my adorable girl, my hands could 'talk' with caresses and we would converse in the most beautiful way in the world. It is something between you and I, darling, something that nobody can ever share.

You have been so utterly wonderful to me in these three years of our 'oneness' but the last twenty months have dragged and wasted themselves. After this 'uncivilised' life it will be so queer to come home again, but your arms around my neck will never seem queer. I will be back and we will live our lovelife just where we stopped. This letter must be a jumble darling 'cos my thoughts have just trickled off the nib, as they came. Even if this were unintelligible, it is only the 'I love you' which counts. Each little word says 'I love you beloved', 'cos I want you. 'Want' is such a big little word and you know all that it means to us.

Goodnight, dearest Cherry, I am passionately in love with you.

Your own Gerald.

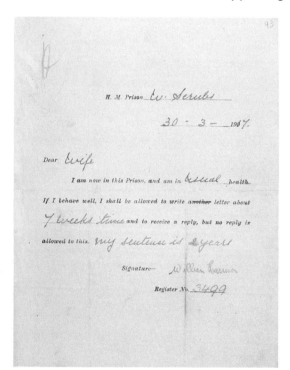

A bleak pre-printed letter sent by William Harrison, a conscientious objector, to his wife Annie, in March 1917 from Newcastle Prison. Some 6,000 COs were imprisoned during the First World War for refusing to fight. The restrictions on communication between these men and their loved ones must have seemed almost more of a punishment than incarceration.

... Hello my sweetheart, it is now 11 o'clock and I have just come to bed. Vern came about 6.30 with some tickets for a show at the concert hall. I went with him and it turned out to be an ENSA show, but quite good. They were most all Scots and a couple of the turns were very poor. There were four chorus girls and goodness, they could dance! They gave an acrobatic dance and I have never seen anything to beat it. What beats me though, darling, is that the Canadians do so much to entertain their boys, the English do so little for their own. If a Canadian wishes he can go somewhere every evening, even with a girl and it costs him hardly anything. There is always something at the concert hall, both in the afternoon and evenings, either a picture or a show very often. On Mondays there is a dance at the Country Club, which incidentally is always open for them and where there is also a film every day. On Tuesdays there is a dance at the Town Hall and tonight they announced a dance for them at Marychurch Town Hall for tomorrow. Oh, and they were also providing transport for them, who wished to go to an ATS dance at Denbury on Thursday. So you see, there is plenty for them to do. I think I like the Canadians much better than any of the others who have been here. Darling, I have been thinking things out a little. We only have a very limited amount of money to spare for entertainment. I think it would be silly to go to concerts. It would be much better to buy records, don't you think, then instead of having the money go on one hearing, we will have the records to hear as often as we like. We can always listen to the concerts on the radio, too, until we have the money to spare. It will be so wonderful when we are in our own home and can get our lives really organised. We can be so happy, you and I. I wish we could have had another Sunny Jim by now if we had had an ordinary life together. I do love you oh so much. Now I must go to sleep or I will never get up in the morning. God bless you, my beloved.

Always your own, Mavis.

Mavis, Gerald and Lesley Ann were not reunited until 1946. Their passion for each other remained undimmed as Mavis explains when she receives a longed-for photograph of her husband:

My beloved,

This morning around 10.30 there was a racket at the door and someone was shouting, 'Where's that Mrs Bunyan?' I rushed out and there was the little postman who handed me, one at a time, six letters from you. He said whilst he was doing it, 'This certainly deserves a hug and a kiss.' I was just going to rush in to start opening them when he shouted, 'Hey wait, that isn't all' and fished in his bag for a package. It was your photograph, darling, and I hardly dared open it in case it was just one of mine you were sending back. Sense told me that you would not send any

Mavis Bunyan treasured these sentimental postcards sent to her by her husband while they were apart.

back by airmail but I was afraid it was too good to be true. I have been such a happy girl all day, beloved. It is a good thing that the pictures do not wear out with being looked at. I cannot describe the feeling it gave me, but as I first looked at it, it was as though you were suddenly in the room with me and my heart seemed to turn somersaults inside me. I almost felt as though, if I put my fingers to your lips, I would feel them so soft and warm. I wanted to touch your face, run my fingers through your hair, as I have done so often in other days. You said it wasn't a good photograph but I think it is the best one there ever was of you.

One of many poems written by Tony Conquest, serving in the Navy, for his wife Peggy:

> You I love and will forever
> You may change but I will never
> Should separation be our lot
> Oh dearest one forget-me-not.

Helen Appleton and Bill Cook fell in love as soon as they first set eyes on each other. He was a young army chaplain soon to be posted to North Africa and Italy, and away from Helen for four and a half years. Much of his pastoral care was concerned with keeping the families of servicemen together: he noticed that homes tended to break up after two years of separation and he encouraged the soldiers who sought his help to keep writing and to keep on trying. He drew his own strength from his faith and from his abundant and loving correspondence with Helen. Their letters, fresh, observant and brimming with love, are a slice of social and wartime history. Helen found herself a job driving tea lorries round the air bases in Norfolk: tea and buns for the British airmen, 'cawfee 'n' donuts' for the US flyers, whom she recalls as free and easy and very attractive. Over the years, she and Bill exchanged 6,000 letters: this unintentionally extraordinary feat is now written up in *The Guinness Book of Records*.

   Here are two of their letters.

From Helen:

10.4.44.
   Easter Day was lovely, with a hectic evening – the Corn Hall was fuller than ever – Mrs B. and lots of valiant souls dished out tea and dried cups while I washed up. Yesterday a crowd of men, passing through, appeared at the Church Hall, while a Bridge Drive was in progress . . . wanting tea.

OPPOSITE: **Keepsakes from Bill and Helen Cook's romance and marriage, including the pens and Bakelite inkwell Bill used out in the Middle East when writing his letters to Helen, his forage cap, Helen's pink crêpe wedding dress, and the photographs of each other they always carried.**

They drank 900 cupfuls before the Canteen was officially open! At 4.30 Dad brought five officers home . . . there was only a tiny piece of cake, so I cut sandwiches – honey/cheese – and gave them quarts of tea. Then I was at Canteen 5.30–10 p.m., men queuing all the time.

Tomorrow a soldier's wife and daughters, aged 7 and 8, come to the Rectory for three days. Mrs P. (evacuee) is still in Thorpe Mental Hospital – she got involved with a Canadian airman, I think, and is mixed up in her mind. Douglas, her four-year-old son, has gone to a children's home temporarily, a friend has taken little Barry.

We had an IOM mother and little girl, and one on the way, staying here, and now a quiet Welsh girl, also expecting. It makes me look forward! But I'm a very happy girl . . . I have the best man in the world and he loves me; and he is doing the very most a chap can do for the Kingdom, he is giving everything all the time. Do you realise how happy that makes me, Bill? To know what great things you are doing just by being you! It is nearly three weeks since I got your 'landed in Italy' airmail so there should be some news to tell all the folk who ask after you each day. God bless you, my Beloved. I love you always.

From Bill:

7.5.44 Sunday evening.

Dearest, Do you remember a year ago today? We ought to have had a Regimental Party to celebrate, but alas nothing is static any more. William and I came to the Sappers tonight for evening services. They are so nice and friendly. We had a happy service, and communion, at the foot of a little hill. It's all rather devastated here, yet spring has come with fields of poppies and flowers of all colours. There are even a few Italians wandering around. At one of this morning's services a woman and a girl carrying baskets of soldiers' washing stopped for communion time, and when it was over they silently placed the little roll of towel on their heads, then the basket, and went away. It was touching.

Another heartbreak tonight. A sapper's sweetie pressed him to get married before he came away from England. They have known each other since they were 15, so they ought to have known their minds. Anyway she has decided that the marriage can't go on. Her letters are vicious. She doesn't want him to come home. What people can do to one another. It will be much easier to beat Hitler than to win the peace and to seek to rebuild in this wreckage of broken towns and homes and lives. Our task is coming clearer and more urgent every day. Sweet dreams, Darling Redhead. I love you always.

Bill married his Darling Redhead in August 1945. Today they are still as devoted and good-humoured as they were then.

For three and a half years after Singapore fell to the Japanese army in 1942, Philip Bloom, a RAMC doctor, and his American-born wife Freddy were separated, but only by a few miles. He was sent to the military PoW camp at Changi on Singapore Island, she was sent to Changi women's civilian prison. Her diary became a letter to Philip, a letter he only read when they were united. In it she wrote detailed descriptions of life in the camp, outlined plans for the future, reflected on life and death. She and Philip had only been married for nine days before they were separated and interned – she was just twenty-eight.

Some of the 6,000 letters exchanged by army chaplain Bill Cook and his sweetheart Helen Appleton during the Second World War.

While interned by the Japanese in a separate camp from her husband Philip for three years, Freddy Bloom kept up a correspondence with him in the form of a diary which he saw only after they were reunited.

4 March 1943.

Interrupted again, darn it, will wait and tell you about our bedroom furniture when we meet. Am feeling very good today; spurning internment, looking forward to the future and getting the most out of the present. Every Thursday morning K and I sunbathe. Today we were a bit harried, for dozens of men's fatigues appeared in all corners and we finally had to sit in a corner of the Infirm Ladies yard where the sun shone somewhat and we played piquet in our bathing suits. At eleven we had a cup of coffee, at twelve stood myself under a tap and now should be doing many things but feel like writing to you instead. Am very fond of Thursdays. Mondays,

Tuesdays, Wednesdays am busy putting out Pow-Wow. Fridays wash and spring clean. Saturday have sketching lesson with Mrs Bateman. Sunday mornings we usually entertain. Tuesday, Thursday and Saturday evenings play bridge. Wednesday evening Shakespeare reading. Monday evening the men's lecture. Tea time these days K and I speak French (mine awful). Tuesday and Thursday afternoon Arts and Crafts classes, Monday and Friday afternoon Braille with Mrs Sherman. Every Saturday night Robbie, Eleanor and I have supper together. The week is highly organised but satisfactory, for it makes the time pass quickly. Day before yesterday it was a year since Fullerton. So far, so good. Even this life has had its moments. Lord, how one learns to savour every little thing that's good. How utterly unaffected one becomes by man's opinions, for one sees how unfounded all those opinions are. One loves humanity in the abstract and certain humans in particular – this love is the essence of living and how one learns to appreciate life. It's good, darling, terribly good – the few miles separating us seem unimportant. I feel so intensely, in fact I *know* we are *living* together.

Later the same day – gotta write some more – am getting such a kick out of life – the wackiness of it all – e.g. the war – such a heap of fuss and bother – everybody going hard at it, killing, destroying, hating and yet look at the haphazard way one gets (not even chooses) one's enemies and allies. Look at the way victories are determined. And then, I suppose, we 'also serve who only sit and wait' – so we grumble about the food and ask for more communication with the outside world. Seriously again, I am often amazed at the hatred and loathing I can feel for individuals and their activities, but I'll be darned if I can hate a race, nation or religion to order. Should I ever devote my life to a cause (apart from you) it would be to the breaking down of this damned national, racial and religious prejudice – war or no war. Fight for your ideals, die for your ideals but never forget what you're fighting and dying for.

Freddy had been much weakened by an attack of beri-beri contracted when she was sent for five months to Kempe-Tai Interrogation Headquarters. There she shared a cell with fifteen men, undergoing appalling deprivation and torture. She survived, and so did her indomitable spirit. Rumours of peace came trickling into Changi in the middle of August 1945, just after she had written this last long entry in her diary to her dear Philip.

5 August 1945.

No letters for me. Life here increasingly irritating as the end comes nearer (what sort of an end, I wonder). Everybody hideously skinny and many of the older people giving in. It might be horribly depressing if it

OVERLEAF: **This album of First World War postcards was bought some years ago in a junk shop. The cards were sent from Walter, a soldier serving on the western front, to his girlfriend Hilda. Intrigued by the increasingly tender messages on the reverse, and wishing to know the outcome of this romance, the buyer went to the records office at Somerset House and found that Walter and Hilda had indeed married after the war ended.**

didn't seem almost inevitable that Singapore be attacked or Japan surrender shortly. On the whole the mortality rate has been wonderfully low. During past weeks I have mended a bucket with latex and canvas, produced footwear out of a defunct football, sewn endless garments with thread pulled out of a sock, cooked most satisfying concoctions from incredible things (we eat most of our flowers. K is most successful with chillies, tapioca – illegal – can be made into almost anything – good, too). Feel capable of tackling any sort of life. Don't know how much of the news is true but the European political situation seems to be solving itself nicely. Labour Government in England is essential now and has come late enough not to be associated only with radicals, ruffians and upstarts. Blum, in France, has always been philosophically in harmony with the present trend and is impractical enough to accept any reconstruction committee's edicts. Of the new American President I know nothing, which seems silly. I am satisfied that regardless of what mistakes will be made (and must be made) they are on the right track with a common aim of international welfare and the strength of will to sacrifice old and dear traditions and sentiments to the general good. I cannot know but I feel that this war was worth fighting (one had one's doubts) and that when we get out we'll find a world worth living in – not as it was after 1918. Am so doggone curious to hear what you want to do. Anything, anywhere! Long time ago wrote a silly poem about 'My husband's my favourite man'. That was after we were parted only a little while. The more I think about it, the more I hear about and see other men (not much chance of the last – still get beaten if caught talking), the more those sentiments stand. What will happen when you actually have your arms around me and I look into those very dear brown eyes and we stand free, in this best of all possible worlds? – Combustion, darling, spontaneous combustion. Will stop this letter. Should anything interesting occur may jot it down in blank pages in front of book. Otherwise no more until we meet.

Desperate anxiety about her boyfriend gave Lucille DesCoteau, an eighteen-year-old American girl, the courage to write this letter to General MacArthur. It was one of many thousands he received:

Lowell, Mass.,
July 30, 1943.
Dear and Brave General MacArthur:

Before you read any further, please ask yourself this question, 'Am I General Douglas MacArthur?' If you are an assistant or mail summariser, you need not read any further. I am sure that you are doing your best in trying to help the greatest man God ever created, but if your answer is 'no' to that question, please deliver this letter *right away* to General

MacArthur because this letter is very important – make sure that *he* gets it right away.

Dear General, by this time you must have my letter, and I beg you, please do not tear it and throw it in the waste basket. Because, in this letter, I want to pour out my heart to you – my own life, I think, could never equal the value of what this letter can perhaps do, so you see how much it means. I know it is very bold and forward of me to write to you – a great General – but my heart is pushing the pen right along and will not let it stop. So, if you don't think you have time right this minute, then put it aside until you do find a few moments – but please read it . . .

My childhood sweetheart and fiancé, Staff Sgt Joseph Roland Dennis Simoneau, enlisted in the Army in 1939. Brave, wasn't he? He lied about his age because he wanted so much to be helping his Country. But, he turned 18 two months later. I will never forget that night – 5 years ago young as we were – I was in my first year of high school – I was fourteen years old – he was seventeen, but we knew our hearts. He said to me, 'Lou, we are too young for love – we must pass this stage of growing up before we can really appreciate what love is; you must continue to be a good girl and I must make a man of myself – we must learn not to be selfish. I want and desire you so much, Lou, and I will work so hard. I will go to school and study hard, and become someone, and I will do everything my Superiors in the Army request of me.' And with those words, he left me . . .

And now I am putting in 48 hours and sometimes 55 hours a week

A fold-out writing set produced for American GIs serving in the Korean War.

working in a War Plant, I still use every minute of my spare time praying for him. He was reported 'missing in action' shortly after the surrender. And, I lived in doubt until three weeks ago when he was reported a Jap[anese] prisoner at a Java camp, by the Japanese Red Cross . . .

But it is him I am fighting for. I do not care if he never wants me when and if he does ever return. All I want is mercy for him. I want him to come back in good health and all in one piece, so that he might enjoy his share of freedom for which he fought. When I hear about how the Jap[anese] treat their prisoners, I can't help but think that *something can be done*. I ask this of you because I have done everything else I could, and I know you are the only one who can do something . . .

I will be 19 in just a few weeks, but please do not think I am a child, because I really am not. I would give my life to save this Country or to save the life of one who fought for it . . .

On my part, I place myself in your full command – anything you ask of me will be obtained – to the last drop of blood I have and my life itself, if you request it. Anything I possess that might help you to get these men out of Java is lying at your feet. *Don't let the Jap[anese] torture these men* . . .

With deep respect, anxiety and love, I am at your command – God Bless you.

Lucille DesCoteau.

1916. Will Martin and Emily Chitticks were sweethearts, but not yet officially engaged. Will was serving with the Royal 1st Devon Yeomanry in Essex and Norfolk. He had been brought up by his aunt, disliked his own mother who had treated him badly and longed for the day when he and Emily could have a home of their own. Each adored the other, although Will, being shy, needed a bit of prodding to approach Mr Chitticks for the hand of his daughter in marriage.

There are seventy-five of Will's letters and twenty-three of Emily's – when men went to France it was difficult for them to keep letters they received safe in the trenches. Will was posted to France early in 1917 with the 8th Battalion, Devonshire Regiment, and their correspondence continued. On 28 March, Emily for some reason started writing in red ink. She did not yet know that her beloved Will had been killed the day before. As was the custom, her letters were eventually returned to her unopened, with 'Casualty: Killed in Action' written on them. Second Lieutenant Caleb, Will's commanding officer, wrote to tell her of his death, as did Will's

OPPOSITE: **Even though she didn't yet know that her fiancé had been killed by a sniper's bullet in the trenches of northern France, for** *some reason* **Emily Chitticks suddenly started writing in red ink the day after he died. Her letters to him were returned to her unopened, marked 'K in A' – 'Killed in Action'. The note in the top right corner was only found after Emily's death years later – too late for Will's letters to be buried with her as she requested.**

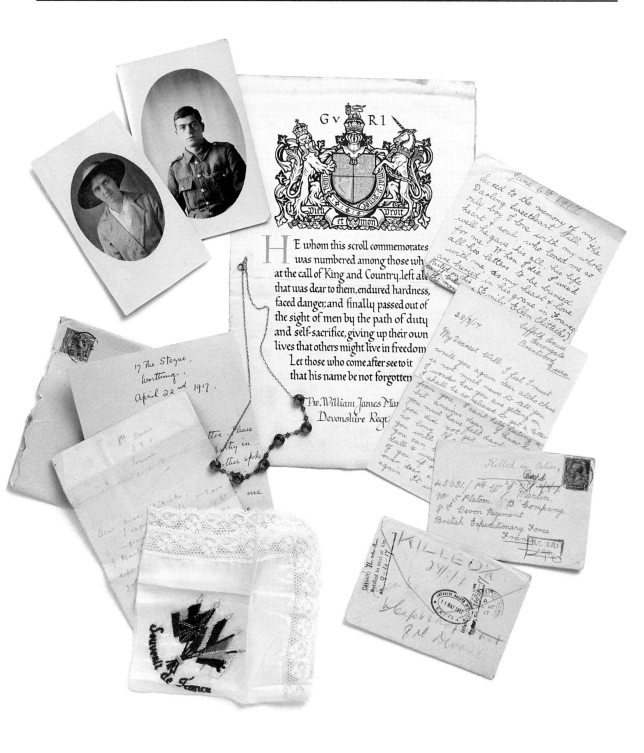

Gv R1

HE whom this scroll commemorates
was numbered among those wh
at the call of King and Country, left al
that was dear to them, endured hardness,
faced danger, and finally passed out of
the sight of men by the path of duty
and self-sacrifice, giving up their own
lives that others might live in freedom

Let those who come after see to it
that his name be not forgotten

Pte. William James Ma
Devonshire Regt

friend Turley; but both Turley and Caleb were themselves killed on 2 April. Emily's letter to Lieutenant Caleb was returned by his sister.

Personal effects of soldiers who had been killed were sent back to the family, an unbearably poignant ordeal for the bereaved. The brief glimpse we have of the destruction of Will and Emily is somehow more shocking because of the courtesy, gentleness and gaiety of their sweet lives.

From Emily:

Best wishes from Mother and Father
Suffolk House
Herongate
Nr Brentwood
Essex.

Thursday even:
My Dearest Will,
    I was so delighted to receive your letter this morning & to hear that you arrived at Witham quite safely. You can't think, dear, how your letter cheered me up. I do miss you terribly, Will, but it won't be for long, will it, dear? so I must try to cheer up until you come back.
    . . . You know I love you, oh so much, Will. You are everything to me, dear, & I don't know what I should do without you, I only wish that this wretched war was over. We shall not have to part from each other so much then, shall we? It was terrible parting from you on Tuesday, Will, I am glad you did not say much to me, as I could not have borne it, dear, I tried hard to be cheerful, Will, for your sake, because I could see that you felt the parting as keenly as I did, & I am sure I should have broken down had you said much to me. I had been dreading & yet longing to see you all day on Tuesday, & I felt, darling, as if every thing that was worth living for had gone from me when you went, but I don't feel so bad about it now I have got your dear letter, I am looking forward for your return. Do you know, dear, altho I have talked to one or two different boys, you are the only one that I have ever loved with my whole heart & soul, & if anything came to part me from you now, Will, I believe it would kill me, I feel more convinced than ever that we are made for each other, don't you, dear?
    . . . Will, it won't be long before Xmas is here now, & we must both try and make the best of things till then. Oh you dear boy, I love you so much & I am so happy because you love me as much as I do you. Somehow, dear,

I don't feel very down, because I know that we both love each other so well, & now that we really belong to each other, well I am about the happiest girl in the world altho of course, darling, it would be so much better if we could be together, but then we can't have every thing our own way, & I really think we have been very lucky indeed.

. . .I say, dear, when you get a chance you might write to Dad, will you, I am sure he would love to hear from you, & you might mention our engagement, dear, as I have been thinking that it will look a lot more respectful towards him if you ask his consent yourself. Of course I know he does agree, but I think it looks better for you to ask him as well. You understand my meaning, don't you, dear? I will send your clothes on to you, dear, as soon as they are ready, but I am going to put a new collar on your shirt first. I can't allow my boy to go with a collar like that. I can make it better for him. Well, my dear Will, I don't think I have much more to say just now, so will conclude with fondest love & kisses from,
    Your Loving Little Sweetheart
        Emily xxxxxxxx

PS Kind regards from Mum and Dad. Write again soon, darling. I love getting letters from you. I could keep reading them all day long.

From Will:

Holt
Norfolk.
My Dearest Emily,
    Just a few lines to accompany the ring, and to acknowledge your letter, dear. It was such a lovely letter, I wish I could write like it, but still we understand. I hope you will like the ring, dear, I tried to get one set with three stones, but I couldn't get the proper size. I will write to your Father, dear, perhaps tonight, but at any rate as soon as I can, I thought about it last week, but I hope you forgive me, dear, when I say that I couldn't summon up the courage, but writing a letter won't be quite such a hard ordeal, and it will be the proper thing.
    . . . Please excuse scribbles, dear, as I am in a terrible hurry. If the ring is too heavy, dear, or if you do not like it in any way, I will get it changed, for I want my girl to have a ring that she would be proud of, please don't forget, will you, dear, it will not hurt my feelings in any way, and now, sweetheart, I will conclude.
    Fondest love and lots of kisses from
    Your Loving Sweetheart
        xxxx Will xxxx
        xxxxxxx

Will to Emily's parents:

A Squadron
R2/1 D.Y.
Holt.
Dear Mrs and Mr Chitticks,

I am writing to ask your consent to my engagement to Emily, & I hope that I shall receive a favourable answer. I don't suppose I need to tell you that I care for her very much, and I know that Emily returns it. At the same time I must thank you very much for the kindness you have shown to me during last week and also while we were at Thorndon Park. I daresay Emily has told you that I am comfortably situated here, which is much more pleasant than everlasting mud.

. . . And as there is no news to tell you I suppose I must conclude with kindest regards,

Yours Very Sincerely,
Will.

The mail always gets through . . . Norman Boyle, serving with the Royal Navy, sent this birthday card from Algiers to his pen-pal sweetheart, Edith, in Liverpool. The ship carrying the card was torpedoed but the mail bag was rescued from the burning vessel and the card was eventually delivered, a little singed round the edges.

From Emily:

My Darling Will,

How can I thank you enough for my dear little ring. I am so delighted with it, dear. I only wish that you were here to put it on for me. It fits nicely, & looks ever so neat & nice on my finger. It's not a bit heavy. You like it yourself, don't you, dear? What a sweet little badge, too. I am so pleased with it, darling, you are a dear kind boy to send me such lovely presents.

. . . I expect, dear, you got some chaffing when those fellows saw that piece of card. I only had one party tell me that I looked very loving in church last Sunday, but I did not mind that. I don't care who knows that I love you, dear, & I feel a very happy & proud girl because you love me. You remember that nice little woman who lives next door here, that told you one night when you were waiting for me that I had gone home, well, dear, she asked after you yesterday, she says she can't help feeling interested in you, as she has seen you so often waiting for me, & she says she thinks you have got such a dear kind face, she has regular fallen in love with your face so I reckon I shall have to hold you tight when you come down here again, don't you, dear? She was so delighted to hear we were engaged, she says 'I am a lucky girl' & I think I am too, dear. I am so proud of you.

From Will:

Your letter gave me a thrill all over, it is such a happy moment to me, sweetheart, when I receive your letters. Yes, dear, I know the person you mean, she used to tell you that she liked me when Mrs Crundle lived at Suffolk House. You will have to hold on tight, dear, when I come home, or else somebody will be attempting to carry me away, and I don't want to see my little girl giving somebody a black eye. I can scarcely understand why so many people fall in love and appreciate me so much. It is quite a new sensation to be thought so much of, but I am glad for your sake. I hope you will always have occasion to be proud of me, dear.

. . . By the way, dear, they asked for volunteers to go to Devonport to train with the 3rd Devons as infantry, and of course go across eventually. I have volunteered for it, but I shall have to pass a medical examination first. It may be cancelled for they do not seem to be in a hurry over it, but if not we shall soon go back to Devon again. I hung back until nearly last, dear, they wanted 17 from our troop and they got 20. In the other troops they will have to draw lots for it for they wouldn't volunteer . . . It is nothing to worry about, dear. Now, Sweetheart, I will close with fondest love & lots of kisses, from

    Your Loving Sweetheart
      xxxx Will xxxx

8th Devons
BEF France 31.3.17.
Dear Miss Chitticks,

    I regret deeply to have to inform you that Pte W. J. Martin was killed on the afternoon of Tuesday March 27th while in the performance of his duty in the front line. He was hit in the head by a sniper's bullet and never recovered consciousness before he died. I am returning to you one or two small things which I found in his pockets and which you might care to keep in memory of him. Believe me, I am extremely sorry to have to give you such painful news, and I deplore his loss, just as do all his comrades in the platoon. Though he had not been with us very long, I found him to be a very keen and capable soldier. Please accept my deepest sympathy in your loss and believe me to be

    Sincerely yours
      C.D.N. Caleb 2/Lt
      8th Devons BEF.

OPPOSITE: **Romantic cards were produced in huge quantities in the First World War. By 1917 the British postal services were handling almost two million postcards and letters a day.**

Miss E Chitticks, Suffolk House
Herongate
Nr Brentwood
Essex.
6/4/17.
Dear Mr Caleb,

I must thank you & also the platoon for your kind sympathy with me in my sad loss. I am very grateful indeed to you for your kindness in writing to me & for sending me those things out of W. Martin's pocket. It is a sad blow to me. I am so pleased to know that you found him a good soldier & that he died doing his duty, with heart felt thanks for your kind sympathy, I remain

Yours sincerely
Miss E. Chitticks
Herongate
Essex.

17 The Steyne
Worthing.
April 22nd 1917.
Dear Miss Chitticks,

I return your letter. Please accept my sincere sympathy in your sad loss.

My brother spoke very highly of Martin & in his last letter to me he told me that he died in his arms. My only brother, the one who wrote to you, was himself killed on April 2nd. So you see how sincere and deep are my sympathies with you.

Yours sincerely,
Gladys Caleb.

She is far from the land where her young hero sleeps
And her lovers are round her, sighing:
But coldly she turns from their gaze, and weeps
For her heart in his grave is lying.

Thomas Moore

— 4 —
BEING APART

SWEET ADELINE (1).

In the evening when I sit alone a-dreaming
Of days gone by, love, to me so dear,
There's a picture that in fancy oft appearing,
Brings back the time, love, when you were near;
It is then I wonder where you are, my darling,
And if your heart to me is still the same,
For the sighing wind and nightingale a-singing,
Are breathing only your own sweet name.

BAMFORTH COPYRIGHT   WORDS BY PERMISSION OF B. FELDMAN & CO.

'I'll be looking at the moon but I'll be seeing you'

Western wind when wilt thou blow
The small rain down can rain
Christ if my love were in my arms
And I in my bed again.

Anon – early 16th century

In the great turmoil of emotions engendered by the war and separation, the spectral queue of fears was headed by anxieties and dreads about the absent lover. Would he or she be true? Would he return home horribly maimed or suffering from shell-shock; would she ever be able to share the nightmare images he had seen? Would the children remember him, and could life ever be normal again? Would it be possible to love again without guilt, and could one forgive and forget infidelity? Wives and sweethearts sat at home while their husbands faced death and had to push the memory of home into the background; husbands and lovers posted to remote corners of the world heard rumours of their women succumbing without a struggle to the charms of richer soldiers on their own doorsteps. Padre Bill Cook:

8.55 p.m. One of our men came up in great distress this evening. He has a wife and child and money saved up for a home, also the prospects of a good job after the war. He had a most hectic battle. I can't tell you about it, but he was lucky to come through, and when he came back to harbour a couple of nights ago there was a letter to say that his Missus had been getting fed up and bored, and playing about with another man. Goodness, this separation is making such a mess. If only he could go home for a leave.

Bill Cook was in Italy, but the same problems appeared everywhere. Ted Cope in North Africa with the Eighth Army was told that it was likely that any leave they were expecting would be cancelled as they were to prepare immediately for another campaign. His feelings bubbled to the surface in his letter to his fiancée, Doreen Roots:

You know you often mention your Canadian cousin Dick. Well, if the Eighth Army ever does come in contact with Canadians I'm certain there'll be trouble. Most people out here have a strong prejudice against them which gets very strong at such times when another chap receives a letter saying that his girl has just thrown him over and married a Canadian. That's pukka, you know – even in our battalion we've had several cases like that. It makes chaps mad out here to think of the Canadians sitting back in England and the Eighth Army training for another campaign. Still it isn't easy to fully appreciate the chaps' outlook here. Their main tick is that you can't always be lucky and get a near miss every time, and they just want to see their people once before the near miss doesn't miss! They aren't scared of another front, but they feel entitled to see their people in the interval.

How on earth can one look forward to a future now when army

OPPOSITE: Copies of this German aerial propaganda leaflet were dropped on Allied troops. Such leaflets played on the vulnerable feelings of men fighting far away from home.

Memorable Moments

THAT lasting embrace of love and affection . . . .

THAT everlasting thought of your return
to your loved one : . . . .

THAT moment of heaven you left behind . . . .

THAT constant wish and hope that all you
hold dear will return SOON . . . .

Does all **THAT** not mean something?

WHAT are your odds in your present
position?

THINK it over **SOLDIER**

THAT can be realized -- by

"SAFETY FIRST"

S K J 2009

commanders reckon the war will last another 3 years? I don't mind, but how can one write with these things on one's mind?

Well, that's eased my mind writing as I have, and now curiously enough I find it easy to write of a future.

You know you mentioned in one of your letters that you had brought something actually for our own home. Was that right? It was awfully nice to think over and certainly gives me a basis for a sane outlook for any future there may be.

How I would wish to spend my life with you in our own home and yet how far away seems the realisation of that wish! I had faith until recently, faith in the future, but we've all been disillusioned . . .

Well, never mind, it will all straighten out, so forget everything and just remember that I love you and that one year, two or three, I shall be wishing all the time just to be with you.

Men England Forgot

Far away across the ocean, lies a land so fair and sweet.
Rugged hills and winding valleys and their homes so small and neat.
Once a land so free and easy, home of England's fighting men,
Now a home for Poles and Frenchmen, Yankies and Canadians.

In towns and country lanes you'll find them there, where we used to
    love and walk.
You can see them boast and swagger, using brave and bragging talk:
What they'll do when they get started, how they'll finish off this war.
What they're going to do with Jerry, but we've heard it all before.

In the meantime, in the desert, far away from sweethearts, and their
    wives,
Britons, rough and ready heroes, fight like madmen for their lives.
Tired, thirsty, scorched and blistered, blinded by the blazing sun,
Half forgotten by their people, in this God forsaken land.

See them waiting every morning, for their highly treasured mail
Knowing what there will be in it, once again the same old tale,
Oh how often I have seen it, seen that agonizing face.
Something in this letter tells him, someone else is in his place.
Can we curse this rank outsider, can we give him all the blame?
Shouldn't these impatient women hold their heads in shame?

I'm not blaming everybody, just these few impatient ones.
In a way they're worse than Jerry, do more harm than all the guns.

OPPOSITE: **The reverse of a German aerial propaganda leaflet.**

So remember wives and 'Sweethearts', when you find you cannot wait,
What your man will have to live for, after he has lost his mate.

After all you have 'Old England',
All the world's most Promised Land,
But without you and our country
ALL WE HAVE IS BURNING SAND.

Anonymous poet serving overseas

The heady combination of uncertainty, imminent mobilisation, possible death and the craving for life-affirming sensations sent marriage statistics rocketing. Affairs of the heart or of the body, however, required no legal permission – they were easier to get into and escape from them needed no lawyers. Men in training camps or overseas could be as unfaithful as they pleased: there were legalised brothels, and prostitution at home and abroad flourished, with its attendant ghouls of disease and degradation. Generally it was accepted that men's appetites needed satisfying, but that women who strayed were sluts. This attitude didn't seem to prevent either side from doing as they pleased.

The magazine agony aunts' postbags were brim full of letters begging for advice and guidance. Men and women wrote about jealousy, infidelity either suspected or committed, marriages under strain. People who had only just met were getting married and parting almost at once as duty called. Some honeymoons lasted only a few hours.

SOLDIER'S WIFE UNFAITHFUL

I am a soldier and recently got 48 hours' unexpected leave. I went home feeling on top of the world but I found that my wife had been associating with another man. I have every reason to believe she has been unfaithful. What ought I to do about it?

Everything depends on how things were before you went away; were you both happy and in love? Is this – if your suspicions are correct – likely to have been a temporary lapse? Talk the matter over now the first shock has worn off – perhaps she could come to where you are stationed. Give her another chance if you feel she has learned her lesson; but, if not, go to your chaplain, he will tell you what legal steps to take, if any.
  Woman's Own, 27 March 1942.

A hand-drawn card sent by Alf Sampson to his wife Renée when he was serving in India and the Middle East. They were apart for four years, but Alf's artistic optimism never wavered.

Alf Sampson sent his wife Renée an illustrated card for each birthday and anniversary they spent apart during the war.

KEEPING FAITH

Please help me, you can't imagine my trouble. My boy has been a prisoner in Japan for three years and I can't go out with other boys when I think of what he may be suffering. All my girl friends are courting now and I am so lonely I don't know what to do.

Poor little girl, it is terrible that this, which should be your happiest time, should be so clouded. But I am glad that you are keeping faith with your boy . . . Isn't there a youth club you could join and make new friends? Or how about volunteering at any local canteen several nights a week?
    Woman's Own, 7 July 1942.

Thirty years earlier, couples who were apart had faced many problems, but the tremendous wave of sexual infidelities didn't exist in the same engulfing proportions. Young Dorothy Roots agonised over the feelings of an unwanted admirer.

In 1917, Dorothy, 'Dodie' to her fiancé Captain Alan Potts, was nursing while Alan served with the British Expeditionary Force in France. They wrote very frequently to each other, although there was a time delay between letters written and received. Dodie was anxious about the attentions shown to her by an injured New Zealander she had nursed. She doesn't mention him in the first letter printed here, but it was obviously on her mind. Being an honest and sweet woman, she had to confess her problem in the second letter.

28/2/17.
2nd Gen Hosp: Chelsea.
    . . . just to see your dear handwriting does me good and puts fresh 'buck' into me always. Darling, you say you trust me, I will try and be worthy, Alan, in all my thoughts, & try to be very true to you & to what I think you would wish . . . Also, and now you will laugh at me, I try to get your mother to talk about you a great deal, all the books you like, all the music, all the people you like or dislike, and what you like *to eat* – very important so I don't give you the wrong things when you come to stay with us and not send things you don't care for in your parcels.
    What will it be like when you are always here and we shall really be together with no horrible haunting fear of separation always hanging over us, but I thank God I have you still, your letters keep coming and I know that somewhere, not so very far away after all, you are there walking about and talking and thinking and being just the same as my remembrance of you . . . One thing you said stuck in my memory all the 15 months you

were away last time, and I kept wondering about you – altogether – and if perhaps I had been wrong about you after all and that someday perhaps you might fall in love with someone; I didn't guess then how ideal your love would be, did I? You said, 'I think when 2 people really love one another and want to be always together it's the most beautiful thing in the world', do you remember, darling, and so it is, isn't it? I do so wonder what the upshot of all this fighting is going to be . . .

3/3/17.

You know that man who gave me the torch for Xmas, well today I have had a letter from him which I gather that some time sooner or later he intends proposing to me. Isn't it dreadful? What am I to do? I must tell you that he has written to me once or twice before, sort of hinting at the fact that he liked me, and he has been back to see us once or twice. I didn't worry much, thinking, you know, that as soon as he got out and about again he would probably forget about it, however it seems he hasn't. I am afraid perhaps I may have been a little to blame over it. I was *fearfully* sorry for him, physically he was such a fine fellow, and just between ourselves they messed him up dreadfully and he knew, then he was always kind and sympathetic to me when I was tired and so on – so naturally I was nice to him. I am awfully sorry about it and I must confess rather frightened, he seems so determined and I don't ever want to see him again, Alan. What shall I say to put him off? It must be something very convincing and of course the difficulties are increased twofold by his being a NZ man, because as I tried to explain to you before, the impossibilities of the whole affair could never be plain to him, and I don't want to hurt his feelings anyway. So don't laugh at me, sweetheart, but advise me quickly what I shall say to him and I shan't write till I hear from you.

Whether she waited for Alan's advice or not, she wrote to poor Duggan the New Zealander. Relieved, she wrote at once to Alan:

11/3/17.

I'll tell you exactly what I have said; I didn't want him to write me any more letters, and that sort of thing in them because tho' it was secret from all but our parents there was someone very dear to me in France and I was certain that person wouldn't like me to have letters like that, and I said I knew he would understand that I felt extra loyal because you were obliged to be so far away from me.

OPPOSITE: **Isolated from women for years on end, prisoners of war desperately needed reminders of femininity. Frank Edwards, imprisoned in Eichstatt camp in Germany during the Second World War, drew beautiful images of girls on posters, leaflets and advertisements for the camp's theatrical productions.**

The German bullet embedded in this clip of cartridges would have killed Company Sergeant Major A W Loveday had the cartridges not taken the force of the shot. He sent this memento home as a reassurance to his beloved wife and baby sons that he would now survive the war. Tragically he was killed by sniper fire in 1918, two months before the Armistice.

Sweetheart, are you *sure* you aren't laughing at me, because it really is a most horrible thing to have happened . . .

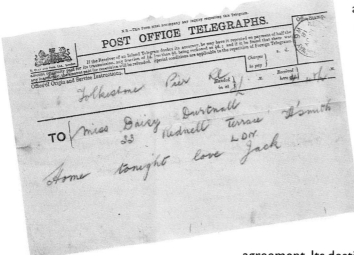

POST OFFICE TELEGRAPHS.

It is not unusual for couples to develop a kind of telepathy, sensing or even experiencing danger or pain felt by the other. Marie-Louise Blackburn was married to a young engineer sent to construct Admiralty Floating Deck 24, an enormous floating dock towed across the Atlantic in June 1943 in three sections by tugs from the USA under the lease-lend agreement. Its destination was Freetown harbour in Sierra Leone. When AFD 24 was completed she resembled a huge block of flats with walls fifty feet above the water and at least fifteen feet below: war-damaged ships would come to her for repairs, which would be undertaken in comparative safety.

A simple message, but in wartime these four words meant everything to the woman waiting at home.

Jack Blackburn and a group of engineers started work on putting the giant dock together. Marie-Louise continues:

One particularly bright summer day in August, at about 2.30 p.m., I suddenly felt very cold with an unusual feeling of fear. My throat became dry and my legs weak whilst a noise like rushing wind raged in my head so that I could not go into my hairdressing salon for the afternoon's appointments. That night I repeated over and over again, 'Jack, are you all right?' and 'Darling, where are you?' It was a great relief when a letter arrived from him, but it was not until he arrived home in November that I heard the whole story.

On that day in August a party of eight engineers working on an end section of AFD 24 were suddenly attacked by a typhoon of such terrifying strength that the huge structure was sent spinning like a top towards the harbour, full of naval anti-submarine ships and would have smashed the ships to matchwood. Jack was the only engineer who understood the valves and when the pilot suggested that the structure would have to be sunk in order to save the ships, he climbed the tower and opened the valves. At that moment, one of the tugs which it had previously broken from managed to get close enough for the men to fix a line, but not before her bridge and superstructure were smashed. Jack hurriedly closed the valves and another tug then came to the rescue and towed it to safety. At last the storm abated: the men and the ships were safe.

OPPOSITE: **This card echoed the sentiments of all those missing their loved ones. During the First World War the swastika, seen in the top left-hand corner, was commonly used as a good-luck symbol.**

Like so many acts of wartime heroism, Jack's exceptional skill and bravery went unrecorded officially. Marie-Louise ends on a reflective note:

Terrible as those years were, they gave us a strength and courage that we did not know we possessed.

A clutch at his war-coat, and our
tear-stained cheeks touch;
The sails must needs be set for the
urgent evening breeze.
Who says, 'For a brief parting grieve not'?
This poor life of mine, how many
brief partings can it endure?

Wan Yen-Hung 1620–1680
Brief Partings III
(tr. Norman L. Smith and Robert Kotewall)

Autograph books were popular in both world wars as a means of remembering friends and fellow servicemen and women. This touching poem was written in a book belonging to **WAAF** radio operator **Linda Collin Wileman.**

To those of us that wait

Not very long .. + will be back with me
And we can wake the dreams that fell asleep
And feel again, the warmth + witchery,
Of every magic rendezvous we keep-- |
He will be changed, but as the days slip past
I know our love can heal the deepest scars,
And if the skies he sees are overcast
Then ill be there to point him out the stars.
          Pam H Warden
In memory of days at Manston

Serving in Italy in 1945, Major Cohen had never seen his two-year-old daughter Suzette when he wrote this adoring birthday letter to her, expressing the yearnings of servicemen everywhere who were missing the young lives of their little children.

My Most Darling Suzette,

This is to wish you many, many happy returns on your birthday. Mummie has written to me that you will have no party to celebrate it because I am still away, but I promise to make it up when I come home, which will not be long now.

Thanks to Mummie I now have a complete picture of your first 2 years of life. You have been an adorable child apart from when you had some new teeth and when you have your hair washed. You have given no trouble or anxiety to Mummie or me but only continual happiness. (Even in the manner of your arrival in October 1943, long, long ago, you caused little trouble.)

Suzette, my Darling, do you think you will love your Daddy whom you have never seen? I hope and think you will, because our whole life is going to be devoted to your happiness. I will throw you into the air, carry you on my shoulder, allow you to cover me with sand, take you into the countryside where Mummie will explain to you and me which are the sheep, which are the cows and the geese and the ducks and the birds and the hens and pigs. We may even if we are lucky (and good) be shewn a squirrel or a deer. You have no idea what happiness is in store for you if Mummie and I have our way, and what happiness you will create for us, too.

You have no choice as to who shall be your daddy, my Darling Sue, because your Mummie has already made the choice, but I hope that you will like the choice. But I'm sure you will – especially when you come into our bed on my first morning back in Southport. That will be an occasion which I shall never forget, we shall have fun and games and that will mark the first day when you start life not only with Mummie but also with me – a real, live, genuine Daddy.

For a few months you will only have us and your grandma and pa to play with, but if you are a very good child we hope to present you with a baby brother whom if you look after carefully for about 12 months will then be ripe to offer you adulation and admiration.

You see, my Darling Sue, you are 'one of the family' – just 3 of us – and as such you are entitled to know all the family secrets.

My whole life is mapped round you and that is why I wish you a very happy birthday.

With all my love and to Mummie,

Your own Daddy xxxx

John Dossett-Davies joined the army in 1945 and after basic training in Britain was posted to Trieste in northern Italy, having been diverted there after the atomic bomb was dropped on Hiroshima. In 1948 he was sent twice to Göttingen, about fifty miles south of Hanover, to study at the College of the Rhine Army. He remembers:

Göttingen was a very pleasant, old medieval town with most of its ancient ramparts still intact. I thought it a very romantic place although I only knew it in the winter and spring. One had a glimpse of the old pre-Hitler Germany in those days when the Gothic script was still in use and local folk costumes were in everyday use. It was the area of Germany where Grimms' Fairy Tales were set, near the Hartz mountains. It was hardly bombed at all. Although I was in Germany briefly in 1945, not long after its collapse, the journey up from Italy through the shattered cities of the Ruhr, with buildings like skeletons, just the outside walls standing, still made a great impression on me; the massive destruction, the poverty of the German people and the harsh winter that year contrasted with the sunshine of the south. There were 60 million refugees and displaced persons moving around, or in camps, waiting to be repatriated or resettled in other continents.

I met Ellen Monnich through an army colleague who was friendly with her sister. We used to meet by the statue of Friedrich von Schiller, the poet, in Göttingen at weekends and when I had evenings off from my studies. Ellen (or Dizzy as I nicknamed her – she called me Jack) was a small, fair-haired girl 18 months older than me – 22. She spoke English quite well and had a very pleasant and melodious voice and would sing German songs to me. We knew each other for almost 2 separate months. I lived out at Weende Barracks (formerly used by the SS, and now I understand a hospital) on the edge of Göttingen, and she lived with her parents, brother and 2 sisters in Leine Strasse near the railway line.

We met as often as we could and went for walks in the woods just outside the town and visited her home and relatives and the cinema. I remember the little house where Bismarck had lived as a student was also a favourite spot for us to meet. The non-fraternisation ban (which banned friendships between British soldiers and German girls) had been lifted by this time. Easter 1948 especially stands out in memory. The weather was very fine and we spent the time together walking and going for picnics.

After Jack's first trip to Göttingen, Dizzy, deeply in love, wrote to thank him for his present of a handbag and to promise a present for his birthday.

Anti-German feeling at the end of the Second World War made it impossible for John Dossett-Davies to marry Dizzy, his beloved German girlfriend.

Göttingen, 15th of Febr. 1948.

My dear Darling Jack,

Many thanks for your most welcome letter which I got today. I am so glad about it. Every day I had look out to a letter from you but the postman said always 'No'. I was very sad because I thought, you have forget me. But Always I look on your photo then I know, you still love me.

The handbag is very nice and I am pleased at it. I think of you as often as I see it. I take it when I go in the theatre but I don't go to the dance when you are not here. It is not good to do that. I miss you so very much and hope I see you again soon. But I walt for you how long you like.

Well, dearest, I hope you got my letter and you are glad about it. I shall send you something to your birth-day and I hope you get it. This letter I give to my sister's boyfriend. He sends it by Forces mail and it goes much quicker. I can read your letter very good and like you writing with the pen.

Dearest, I like the new Name you find for me but let me know your address in England in your next letter, please, perhaps you forget it later.

The spring starts now. The birds sing and the flowers come out. In the afternoon the sun shines and I see the young people go for walk with their love. Only I can dream about it. But when you come to me again, it is Springtime for me.

I close now and go in bed and dream about you. Lots of love to you from your ever loving,

xxxxxxxxx Dizzy.

xxxxxxxxx

xxxxxxxx

xxxxxxx

xxxxx

xxxxxxxxxxxxxx

John was very fond of Dizzy — she was his first serious girlfriend, certainly the first he had really been in love with. He took food to her family to keep them going when Germans were severely deprived — he remembers drinking excruciating acorn coffee; the US army blanket he had given them was quickly tailored into an elegant lady's costume. After his second visit faithful Dizzy continued writing:

Göttingen, 9th of May 1948.

My dear Jack,

I am sorry because I had no letter from you for the last 14 days and I look so much forward to get some lines from you. Otherwise I have every weekend a letter.

Well, dear, what's the matter? Do you still well? I am and my family also. Or do you have too much to do? I want a letter from you, please.

Did you get my letters? I hope it. Do you like the ring? It costs not very much but it will remind you at me. I hope, you think often at me.

Well, dear, write to me soon, I wait for some words of you.

I close now. I am always thinking of you.

Regards and kisses from

your loving

Dizzy.

xxxxx

xxxx

As Helena Meijers said goodbye to her English sweetheart, Reginald Blannin, at the end of his leave, he smoked part of a cigarette and with a kiss gave it to her. She has kept it all these years, together with the colourful letters she wrote before they finally married in 1946.

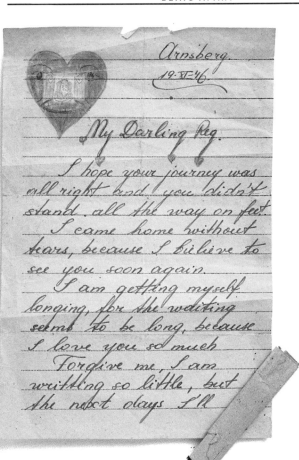

Arnsberg.
19·XI·46.

My Darling Reg,

I hope your journey was all right and you did'n't stand all the way on feet.

I came home without tears, because I believe to see you soon again.

I am getting myself longing, for the waiting seems to be long, because I love you so much

Forgive me, I am writting so little, but the next days I'll write more.

My thoughts are always with you and the very most at ten o'clock.

I am for always yours Helena

Good Night!
Reg.

"How long have you got Fred?"

"LEAVE"

The time came when John had to return to England. Although he fully intended to send for Dizzy in due course and to marry her, he hadn't realised how anti-German the feeling was in post-war Britain.

Even close friends and relatives were rabidly anti-German. Again, of course, the newness of release from the army and adjustment to civilian life meant that memory of my German girlfriend began to fade. I didn't however have another girlfriend until 2 years later. I think the moment I realised it was over was when a cousin of mine, a major in the Royal Artillery, told me of his friend who wanted to marry a German girl. 'One of the enemy,' he called her. 'I'll never speak to him again,' he said. I didn't tell him of my relationship, but felt I couldn't go on with it.

John wrote to Ellen to tell her that their love affair was over. Dizzy wrote one last distraught letter, unable to believe it, promising she would love him forever, would never forget him. They never saw each other again; but John has kept all her letters and the ring she sent him. Forty years later, he wrote a poignant poem about their time together:

> Ellen – Germany in the Spring
> Easter 1948.
>
> We lay in the Hartz woods,
> The fir trees above us
> Like the masts of sailing ships.
>
> The tiny German fraulein
> From old Göttingen
> Who spoke beautiful English
> And had a delicate air.
> I was a soldier/student.
> She was trying
> To stay alive
> In a shattered Europe.
>
> She taught me
> Of life and love
> And Bismarck and Beethoven,
> My gifts kept her family alive.

'Sweetheart' brooches, many incorporating a regimental badge, were produced during the First World War and worn by the wives, girlfriends and mothers of servicemen.

She gave me a ring,
I gave her cloth,
She recited Schiller
While I drank acorn coffee in Leine Strasse.

In 1988, Margaret Semple, born in 1890 in Adlington, Lancashire, was visited by Margaret McGrath, her niece and namesake. The younger Margaret was about to return to Australia where she now lived. It was to be their last meeting, although neither knew it at the time. Aunt Margaret Semple extracted from her niece the promise that she would return to sort through and tidy up the old lady's belongings when she was finally gathered in.

Margaret McGrath visited England again a year later, after her old aunt had died. She kept her promise and started to sort through the great collection of belongings left to her. She was startled to find a different kind of person revealed from the ancient white-haired maiden aunt she had known. In two cabin trunks and three suitcases strung up with rope were . . .

. . . photos and uniform from her service in the 14–18 war. Charleston chiffons and gold shoes, from early cosmetics to an unopened box of Lux Soapflakes at 4d. Beautiful white lace camisoles, knickers to the knees and longer! Lace upon beautiful lace and yet more lace, snow white and folded in tissue as perfect as the day it was stored away. The 1920s tennis dress she had promised me when I was at school 40 years ago and it would have been old-fashioned then, and yet now looked strangely 'in fashion'. A brush and comb and even a matching buttonhook with a silver hand, packets of hairclips.

A soldier in the trenches made this cigarette-lighter in the trenches and engraved his initials and those of his girlfriend on the hexagonal sides. She kept it as a treasured memento after his death.

There were letters, too – boxes, packets, bundles, attaché cases, bags, all filled with letters, postcards, photographs and cards. They took a while to sort and catalogue. It was after midnight when Margaret decided to open one of the three small attaché cases:

Inside was a white linen bag tied with a draw-string. The initials M.S. on a name tape were stitched on the inside of the bag. The top had a band of drawn threadwork and a white

spray of leaves was embroidered on the front. These must be special, I decided. There were 70 letters inside in various types and sizes of envelopes and they all bore one signature, 'Jock'.

Jock McLeod and Meg Semple had been childhood friends; both attended the same Congregational Church at Adlington. They used to go for long walks together and when Jock joined the Black Watch he and Meg wrote to each other. Meg knitted for him and sent parcels. His letters were ostensibly friendly and chatty; only one of Meg's has survived, and that was one returned to her when he had been posted to Belgium. She must have been very much in love with him, even though he often failed to keep arranged meetings with her. Her letter shows her as a spirited and light-hearted girl. Her dejection when he writes his last letter is evident in the draft note she prepared in reply.

6 August 1915.
Invergordon, Thursday.
Dear Meg,

Awfully sorry I was unable to write sooner, but since my promotion last week I've not had a moment to spare; but I'm enclosing one of my Photos as a Peace Offering! In the hope, of course, of receiving one of yours in return.

I've just received a letter from my brother in Armentières (or should I say 'Somewhere in France'?) – he has come out of the trenches again. He says it's fine watching our artillery blowing up the Germans & further remarks 'that we seem to have plenty of ammunition now'. He asks if I can't join him yet, & I've replied that I'm only waiting the word. I wish I could join him & see what real modern warfare is.

I can't understand how the stamp got in my last letter, Meg; I must have left it in my writing pad at some previous time. Did you think it was a gentle hint to write sooner?

I received the lettercard, of course, & the Photos now adorn the walls of the bunk & make it look more homelike & cheerful, & I herewith return thanks for same. And besides, it was the only way of keeping it! Some fellows, you know, are inflicted with kleptomania when in Camp! As you surmise Invergordon *is* a compact place, merely a large village clustered round the pier.

It consists of one wide street, with smaller streets running off on each side. The *Queen Lizzie* is lying here now. The crew, with their band, was out for a march this morning: just in front of us. Do you really mean it, Meg, when you say you're coming on a 'flying visit'?

Jock and Meg met and started writing to each other in 1915. To Jock, Meg was a dear friend to whom he sent cartoons, postcards and lively funny letters; to Meg, he meant everything. But the relationship was not to last. Meg never married and on her death all his seventy letters were found carefully wrapped in a linen bag and hidden in a small case.

You'd get a 'Cameron Body Guard' all right in Inverness, but we poor beggars up here are not allowed out. The Camerons in Inverness are 'terriers'. They wear leather belts & sporrans.

I got the stripe easily enough, & a lot of work to do too! We've got 105 Sergeants but we are short of Corporals, & altho' we've more NCOs than any ordinary Batt, we've got our work cut out, I assure you. We get two drafts of recruits per week, you see, and in six to eight weeks they're away to the front. Pretty quick work, eh?

The Fleet went out the other night after a submarine and there was heavy firing, but the beastly thing escaped. Hard cheese!

It's an education to be in a Regular Batt. I never knew how strong discipline was before until I came up here. And they're so strict, too. All Highland Regts except ours wear the belted kilt; we still have the ancient method of three long pins only. No excuse is accepted for being improperly dressed. This is how the uniform has to be worn – the kilt to reach centre of kneecap and to be half an inch lower at the back. Left apron to fold over the right and pinned at the right side. Yellow stripe or Tartan in centre of tunic. Hose one inch above centre of calf, double dice at back. One hand's breadth between kilt and hose. Garter tails 5.5 inches long, 3.5 inches to show below the fold. Two on each side, one inch from centre. Garters to be fish-tailed. Spats made for each man and to have eight buttons: boys seven. Shoes only to be worn. Tunic cut away in front for sporran or apron. Glengarry to be worn one inch above right eye and one inch above right ear. Cap ribbons same length as cap (or Glengarry). Rosettes only worn by Officers, NCOs, Band and Pipers. Same applies to Tartan Trews and Staff Buttons.

Now what d'you think of that? Then again, the 'Campbells are coming' is *never* heard in the Camerons, and is forbidden to be played, as the Campbells helped to massacre the Macdonalds at Glencoe and the Camerons and Macdonalds are related.

The Cameron Band never plays going to church, only coming back – I forget why!

The pipers are always men from 'ta Hielants' and they're a queer lot, too. We'd one in our Hut, and if he woke up in the night instead of having a smoke he'd have a tune on the Pipes! He never required any persuasion to play! It gets hold like a bad habit. We're a wonderful crowd!

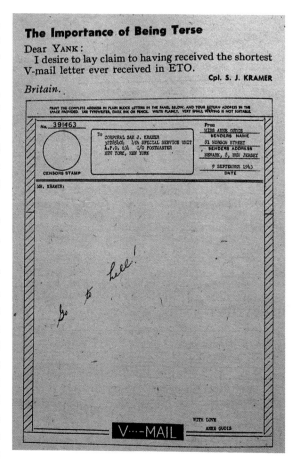

The Importance of Being Terse

Dear YANK:
   I desire to lay claim to having received the shortest V-mail letter ever received in ETO.

Cpl. S. J. KRAMER

Britain.

In 1943 a disgruntled GI sent *Yank* magazine what he claimed was the shortest V-Mail letter ever received. It simply said: 'Mr Kramer: Go to hell! With love, Anne Gudis.' As it turned out, Samuel Kramer seemed to deserve such a rebuff, but before her side of the story could be told, poor Anne received massive public criticism for failing to show due regard for the upkeep of a soldier's morale. The couple eventually patched up the wounds and were married in November 1945.

OPPOSITE: **Railway stations provided the backdrop to many emotional partings in wartime.**

Winter is drawing in now and it gets chilly up here at night, and winter rations are being issued.

Well, Meg, Tempus *does* fugit, so I'll come to a finish hoping you're A1 and thanking you in anticipation for the Photo!

I remain,

Yours sincerely,

Jock

17145 Lce Corpl McLeod

A Coy 3. Camerons.

The following letter was returned to sender marked PRESENT LOCATION UNCERTAIN:

3, Gabbot St

Adlington

Lancs, Eng.

Nov 30 1915.

Dear Jock,

Twenty-five, today! Tempus *does* fugit! – for I can hardly realise that I've lived twenty-five years. And yet, but then I needn't repeat the old adage, need I?

Very many thanks for your most interesting epistle, to hand this morning! I'm delighted that the parcel received such approbation; the helmet, please sir, is still 'on the needles', and so, my dear boy, just possess yourself in patience and in due course you shall see – *what you shall see!*

Well, Jock, you're on the 'war-path' with a vengeance now – and have had some narrow escapes, too! Quelle chance! (for which praises be!) Would that this unspeakable war, with its attendant strife and chaos, and all the gnawing anxieties that inevitably follow in its wake, were over. But it's of no use whining; there are too many 'whimperers and bleaters' as it is. One needs to be as philosophical as possible these days.

No, you didn't tell me about the German plane dropping on one of your dug-outs! So you may proceed with the narrative – ad libitum – of course – and I'll promise you rapt attention.

That reminds me, I should imagine that you will have a splendid opportunity for perfecting your French, now – pardon! – I mean acquiring the correct accent – cela va sans dire! eh, Jock? Apropos, should you contemplate taking any pupils 'by the hand' in future, you won't forget *this ignoramus*, will you?

Now, I'm about to ask a great favour of you, (keep cool, please!) are there any high-spirited horses and shining swords to be had in your vicinity for the price of half-nothing? If so, do, for pity's sake, send me one of each post haste. You see, I've just been seized with a great desire to see

Life in its fullest measure – free, boundless Life!!! An acquaintance of mine, a 'young Chorley hopeful', now training in Ireland, writes that he 'wouldn't like to be in the infantry'. 'For,' says he, 'you don't realise life at all, until you go flying along as fast as the horse can go, with a shining sword in your hand. You forget everything; even Chorley is forgotten in the mad rush!' What blissful ignorance! I should dearly love to 'say a few words to him', but will spare him – lest I damp his ardour.

Quite a number of our village lads are having trench furloughs, so we hear 'some' tales, I can assure you. Has Will volunteered – 'in his class' yet, or is he 'starred'? I've seen him several times in Bolton of late, but not to converse with.

With best wishes,

Most sincerely yours,

Meg.

12th Casualty Clearing Station
Sunday 12.12.1915.
Dear Meg,

Since my last letter to you I have not had a line or word from Home, owing to the fact that I'm still in hospital with my damaged leg, and no letters have come here, so I'm writing again to let you know that if you replied to my last letter you'll understand why I haven't replied to yours. Compri, Mam'selle?

The Hospital I'm in appears to be a College or something for senior boys, and Priests, apparently, are in charge. It is a very large building in the centre of a French town, and a large part of it is in use for a Hospital & Dressing Station. I am bound to confess we are very well looked after, and fairly comfortable, as things go out here. We get the daily papers (for the preceding day, of course) every morning, price 2d! Most of the cases in here are suffering from 'French feet', a form of frost-bite, apparently. I had a touch of it myself and don't want any more. It's caused by standing for days up to the knees in water. Imagine, if you can, going out tonight and standing for twelve days and nights in some drain or ditch up to the knees, the only exercise being in walking up and down, and you'll get some idea of what it's like. It's not so bad when one has Gum Boots, only, even they get wet inside sometimes. When we came out last time the 'Allemands' gave us some fine music by their brass band, played 'God Save the King' and other favourite tunes!

We are only about 25 yds off them, and often we saw their working parties going about, and they lit big fires and clouds of smoked rolled over, but let us light a fire and we'd be shelled out of it in no time!

Many a time I've been out to visit the 'Listening Post' and heard them talking, laughing, and singing as if there wasn't a Tommy within fifty miles!

Our Division, the 9th, comes out for the 'Rest' on the 24th. We'll be in billets in some French town for a few weeks, I expect. We'll leave the trenches on Xmas Eve, you see.

I expect all letters for me will be lying up at Headquarters, so when I go back this week I'll have a few letters to read, and write replies to! Well, Meg, I've no news to send, but hope I'll get a letter from you shortly again, so I'll conclude hoping you're still having a good time.

Sincerely yours,
Jock.

In his last letter to Meg, Jock tells her of his love for a nurse and asks for her forgiveness.

No 8 Clearing Station,
Friday 11.2.1916.
Ward 6.
Dear Meg,

Did you get my Field Card stating I was wounded? I was shot thro' the right breast just a fortnight ago and am only now able to sit up and write.

The bullet struck the parapet and flattened before it struck me and so made rather a nasty wound.

I am going on very well, altho' the Doctors did not remove the bullet.

I am expecting to be sent down to the Base at any moment now. It was very curious that I'd just given up the strip and gone to 'A' Co'y, and got hit!

I think the enclosed address will find me all right, Meg, so I'll close, with kind regards,

Sincerely yours,
Jock.

Northumberland War Hospital,
Gosforth,
Newcastle-on-Tyne.
23.3.1916.
Dear Meg,

I arrived here this morning about three o'clock, after a terrible journey, from No. 1 Canadian Hospital at Etaples, where I stayed six days. I left Etaples at five thirty yesterday morning, sailed from Calais at twelve noon, and arrived Dover two thirty, after a rough passage. When one is badly wounded it's awful being shifted from Motor Ambulance to Ambulance, Train then on to Hospital Ship, back in the train, then on to Motor and finally carried half a mile on the stretcher. I was in a state of collapse!

However, I'm back in good old Blighty again and that's the great thing. Très bon, Mam'selle!

Well, Meg, drop me a few lines and let me know how you're getting on, as I've not heard from you for weeks. Hoping you're in the best of health and trusting to hear from you shortly.

I remain,
Yours sincerely,
Jock.

8 Ju 1917.
Wireless Testing Park
Biggin Hill
Westerham, Kent.
Dear Meg,

Thanks for yours to hand yesterday, and sorry to hear they make you work such long hours. You must be 'fed up' now. You're lucky to have such a chum tho'. I had a letter from Will the other day, and he says he's up in the trenches now, facing Fritz, and dodging all sorts of things.

I've not heard any more from the GPO yet, so I'll drop them a line to tell them where, and how, I am now-a-days, I think.

But there's something I want to tell you about, Meg, something which I didn't mean to ever tell you, but now feel I must tell.

I expect you'll think all sorts of things about me, but it's better to know now than when too late, so I'll tell you everything.

Well, when I was in Hospital I met a Nurse there, and we became very friendly, and it wasn't long before I realised how much I was in love with her, so I told her and found that she also cared for me, but, alas, she'd sworn never to marry owing to a weak heart, due to rheumatic fever or something; and nothing I could say or do would make her relent, but she promised always to write and let me know how she was getting on, and she writes yet, but never a word of love or anything of course. So I gave it up in despair, and then you came along and I forgot – but not for long, however. Try as I might she remains with me just the same, and won't be forgotten. So, altho' you know how much I like and respect you, you can see how hopeless it is for me to really care for you as I ought to. I'm sorry, Meg, Heaven alone knows how sorry, but I won't stand in your light any longer and spoil your other chances.

I can only hope you'll meet some boy who'll love you as you deserve to be loved, while I must just go on hoping and waiting that some day she'll want me and forget all the rest. I've not asked her again since, of course, for I not only knew it was no use but as I said before, I hoped I should have no desire to. I know how cruel I've been to you, Meg, but try and forgive me, and tell me what and how I should do now. Won't you write and tell me, please? If I don't hear from you again I shall conclude I've offended past all forgiveness; but you'll know how Fate treats me if ever you hear of me being engaged, or getting married, for I'll never marry any but this one girl.

So I'll conclude, Meg, hoping I may ever sign myself,
Your sincere friend,
Jock.

13.6.17.

The heart is not of me to 'tell you what you must do'. May Fate one day grant you your heart's desire, and Time be good enough to help me endure and survive this bitterness.

Meg may or may not have sent this brief note. She put the draft for it together with all Jock's letters and hid them away in the little linen bag.

Meg drafted this last reply to Jock, her heartache showing in every word.

"I WONDER WHO'S KISSING HER NOW?"
"Savoir qui l'embrasse en ce moment."

A Donald McGill postcard echoing the age-long worry of soldiers separated from their sweethearts. It has been calculated that in the Second World War the years of life spent abroad by the men of England and Wales totalled an astonishing five million.

Separation in War

I dare not hope such love as once was ours.
Sorrow heaped on sorrow deadens sorrow;
The heart must have relief. Each day that dawns
Draws me further from you, dims the vision
That once before my eyes was all delight,
Dulls the dream that once was all my duty,
Destroys the happiness, dilutes the hope,
Saps the courage and the certainty;
Within the garden of expressed desire
Tears, deracinates the blossomed rapture
And lays accomplished years of love to waste.
You, who were once my lover, have become now
A name, a memory, a cherished thought,
An entity as faint as my lost childhood.

J G Meddemmen
1941

PARTINGS

'Ev'ry time we say goodbye'

The flowers left thick at nightfall in the wood
This Eastertide call into mind the men,
Now far from home, who, with their sweethearts, should
Have gathered them and will do never again.

Edward Thomas – *Easter 1915*

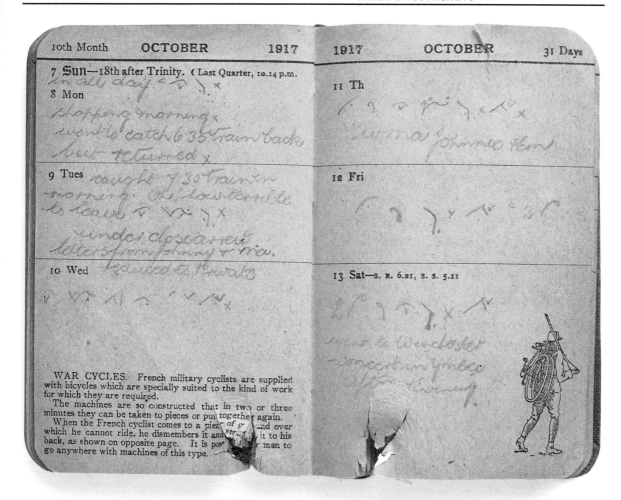

William Merryweather (opposite) kept this diary in which he recorded in shorthand his meetings with his darling Betty. The hole in the diary was made by the bullet that killed him.

William Merryweather, a studious and bookish young man, joined up as a rifleman in the London Regiment in 1916. He knew shorthand and used it for many of the entries in his little *Soldier's Own Diary*. Keeping a diary in wartime in the services was illegal, but so many did it that it grew to be merely frowned on. However, this makes it more remarkable that young William's diary was returned to his family at all. It was found on his body, torn by a bullet, at Cambrai in northern France in 1917. From the pages emerge the feelings of desperate love he harboured for Betty, although all else about her remains a mystery. Her name appears every day: 'my Betty', 'my beloved Betty', 'my darling'. He recorded the letters he received from her and those he sent, and, in the tiny space the diary allowed him, what his military duties were that day. Over the weekend of 7 and 8 July 1917, he was with Betty.

7 Sat. Parade 7–8 9–12.30. Saw my darling at 2.15 p.m., went to pictures in the evening with her and Violet. Letter from Dad.

8 Sun. Church Parade 9.30. With Betty at 12.45. Stayed to dinner and tea and supper.

9 Mon. Parade 7–8 9–2. With Betty at 5.30. Told her I was going away Wed. Terrible shock to my darling.

When he returned to his barracks, Betty saw him on to the train at Frinton and they wrote to each other two or three times daily. On 1 October the entry reads:

3 letters from my love. Replied. Promoted L/Sgt.

With his new sergeant's stripes on his shoulder, he went to see Betty on the 2nd: Oh! What a meeting.

For the next four days he and Betty were inseparable; they stayed in, went to the theatre, had photographs taken. William wired the camp to ask permission for an extension to his leave; it was not granted. After the weekend, on the 8th:

Went to catch 6.35 train back, but returned.

9 Tue. Caught 7.30 train in morning. Oh, how terrible to leave my beloved Betty. Under close arrest.

10 Wed. Reduced to Private. My beloved wrote to me and I replied.

A week later, having sent a further two letters and a card from Southampton, he embarked for Le Havre. At each stop they made on their journey down through France – Rouen, St Pol, St Eloi, Cauchy-la-Tour – he wrote or started letters to his beloved girl.

When his few personal belongings were sent back after his death, the usual medals were amongst them; although he had been demoted so swiftly for being Absent Without Leave, the little diary is a truer testament to his character and love than the medals and his erstwhile sergeant's stripes.

When Stephanie Batstone joined the Wrens in 1942 she applied to train as a visual signaller. In a test taken halfway through her training she showed remarkable proficiency, gaining 89 per cent for her written paper and full marks for practical morse and semaphore.

OPPOSITE: **A soldier and his sweetheart say goodbye, not knowing when or if they will be together again.**

Commander Worsley Gibson RN wrote this loving last letter in 1915, just before going into action, intending it to be sent to his wife in the event of his getting, as he put it, 'bowled over'. He survived the war, becoming a Rear Admiral, and the letter remained unopened among his papers.

She was posted to the Ganavan War Signal Station on the west coast of Scotland.

After the war she wrote about an encounter which nearly took place between her and an Aldis-lamp operator on a decrepit US ship, one of many, some quite badly damaged, which had sailed into the anchorage in May 1944. The ships had no radio contact with the shore, and their only link to land was provided by the Wren signallers:

[I was] glued to the Aldis day and night, no time for a cup of tea. One morning I was getting desperate, with another ten signals to send before Jill came to relieve me in half an hour, and a US merchantman tucked behind another one who couldn't see my lamp or didn't choose to answer. To make things worse, the ship in front started calling me up.

I ignored it for a bit and then sent him the equivalent of 'What do you want, curse you, can't you see I'm busy?' as fast as I knew how. Almost too fast to read, came back, 'I know – can I relay your signals? – the guy behind me can't see your lamp.'

Thankfully I loaded a backlog of signals on to the obliging signalman and made a mental note that No 560, the *Matt W Ransom*, was a useful relay ship.

At the end the signalman flashed, 'When you have time, will you call me up? Name of Jack.' 'OK,' I said.

In the middle of the night there was a lull for a bit, and Jack must have seen the lamp wasn't flashing and called me up. From then on, that curious relationship, which is only possible by lamp, developed. As the light

For many wives and sweethearts awaiting news of their menfolk, the arrival of a bluntly-worded telegram confirmed their worst unspoken fears. Winifred Probst received the news of her husband's death in September 1943. After such a notification it would often take months to discover the circumstances in which a loved one had died.

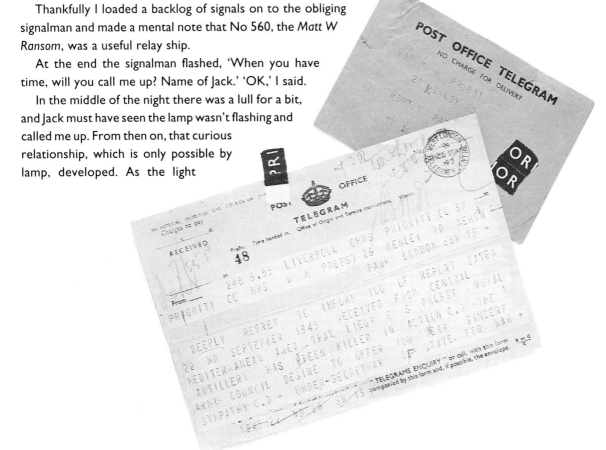

Communicating only by means of an Aldis lamp, Wren Stephanie Batstone built up a friendship with an American signalman, Jack Campbell. To this day she does not know if he survived the war or if he died blowing up a blockship in 1944.

flickered back and forth across four miles of Scottish sea, spirit reached out to spirit, and a kind of rapport of shorthand grew, both of us knowing we were signalling so fast and abbreviating so much that nobody else could read our morse. At its best, this form of communication is far superior to speech, with the added advantages that it can be broken off at any suitable moment, and that imagination supplies the visual image – in this case Jack who, he assured me, was tall, dark and handsome and came from Ohio, and me, who he fondly saw as cute and charming – in fact the pin-up girl of the *Matt W Ransom*. At the end of the day – 'Kiss me goodnight', then 'Mmmmmmmm – that was lovely – another. Gee, you're terrific.'

Jack wrote to me, so he said. When I got the letter, I was to reply with a photo (which would probably have put paid to the pin-up dream). Surely it wouldn't take long for the letter to come four miles. But I waited and waited and it didn't come.

On May 31st, as I climbed up the cliff at 0800, I saw that the anchorage was empty – every ship had sailed. The night watch told us, 'They went at dawn.'

Although Stephanie Batstone didn't know it at the time, the ships, loaded with explosive charges, had sailed to the artificial harbour – the famous Mulberry Harbour – just off the French coast near Arromanches. They were to be sunk there – fuses set and the crews to abandon ship in just four minutes before the detonators were timed to go off.

On July 13th I was woken up from my sleep after night watch by Ann. 'There's a letter,' she said. 'It's got an American Red Cross on the back of the envelope. It says on the front, sender Signalman J C Campbell.' It had taken two months to come four miles.

Breathlessly I wrote a reply, enclosed a photo, and posted it. But there was never a second letter from Jack.

I asked everyone I could think of in the Base what had happened to the crews of the blockships. 'Oh well,' they said, 'it was a risky job, you know, it was difficult to get the crews off, once they'd blown up their ships. Some of them had to stay aboard. Anyway, they were all volunteers.'

For years after I used to imagine the doomed voyage of the last big convoy out of Oban, all down the west coast of Scotland and England and across the Channel, and wonder how it felt, for men whose lives were bound up in pride in their ships, to have to blow them up so near to the

Recruitment posters of this type portrayed the strong wife and mother able to cope with the prospect of her husband going off to war.

Sunday 4th Oct. 1942.

My Darling little Pat,

I have been thinking things over while waiting for my up. boat, & as I might not return, I think it is only right that you should have a letter from me which you can keep, to remember me by. I am writing this assuming you are now grown up, as you will not receive this till then.

I can picture you as a lovely girl, very happy with plenty of boy friends. I am finding it very hard to write this as I may never see you in this stage. You have always been the pride & joy of my life. I have loved you more than my life at all times. As mother has told you perhaps I was always afraid of losing you.

till you get the right one. Remember me as your dad & pal who worshiped the ground you walked on. Please don't do any thing that will upset mother, as I shouldn't like you to. I will close now my little ray of shine. Always loving you.

Your Loving

Father.

XXXXXXXXXXX

Frederick Baker's touching letter to his four-year-old daughter Patricia, written in 1942, to be opened in the event of his death. He was killed in the Dodecanese in November 1943.

enemy and then not be able to get away. And I will always wonder whether Jack Campbell is alive and well and living in Ohio or if he is lying beneath the remains of the Mulberry Harbour.

Poem

The stolen, crowded moments fly,
Too fragile is this breathing space;
Too soon his eager frame must lie
Forlornly in some foreign place;
My heart cries out that he will die,
And I have never seen his face.

For these few weeks he wanders free,
Yet dimly comprehends the choice
Which he has made, forsaking me;
No memories my hours rejoice;
A world of silent grief I see,
For I have never heard his voice.

Bitter it is that he must die,
Before our love was young and glad;
Yet though I know that, in him, I
Must lose the things I never had,
Harder it is to feel that he
Will never know those things in me.

Stephanie Batstone

Instead of sending postcards or photographs Frederick Baker made scores of drawings of scenes in North Africa where he had been posted, which he sent home to his wife Ruby. 'My darling wife,' he wrote on each, followed by descriptions of the scene, enquiries about his beloved family and ending 'All my love', 'Remember I love you', 'Keep smiling'. On one drawing he did from memory of his two children he wrote, 'Do they still look something like this, love Ted!' In 1942 he wrote special letters to each child and to his wife to be opened if he never came back; in the case of the children, to be kept until they were old enough to understand. He was posted to the Dodecanese where he was killed on the island of Leros. Patricia, his daughter, was four years old. This is the letter he had written to her:

Sunday, 4th October 1942.

My Darling little Pat,

I have been thinking things over while waiting for my boat, and as I might not return, I think it is only right that you should have a letter from me which you can keep, to remember me by. I am writing this assuming you are now grown up, as you will not receive this till then. I can picture you as a lovely girl, very happy with lots of boy friends. I am finding it very hard to write this as I may never see you at this stage. You have always been the pride and joy of my life. I have loved you more than my life and at all times. As mother has told you perhaps, I was always afraid of losing you. Now the tables have turned the other way and I might be the one to get lost. But do not let this upset you if this is the case, as the love for a father only lasts up to the time a girl finds the man she wants and gets married. Well, darling, when this time arises I hope you find the right one and he will not only be a good husband to you, but will also make up for the fatherly love you have missed. At all times, lovie, be a pal to mother and look after her, do what you can to make her happy, as she has been and will always be, I am sure, the best little mother you will find on this earth. Don't be selfish or catty, remember there are others in the world as well as you. Try not to talk about people as this gets you disliked. When the pulling to pieces starts, walk out or turn a deaf ear, it will pay in the long run. Above all I want you to be a sport, to take up swimming, dancing and all the games in life you can get so much fun out of. Mother, I am sure, will do her best for you and see you get all the instruction she can afford. Always try to be a sister to Peter and John, they may pull your leg about different things. But the best way after all is to ignore them and do what you can for them. You will win in the end and be the best of pals. Well, darling, there is no more I can say, but to look after yourself where men are concerned, be wise and quick witted and only believe half they say, of course till you get the right one. Remember me as your dad and pal who worshipped the ground you walked on. Please don't do anything that will upset mother, and I shouldn't like you to. I will close now, my little ray of sunshine.

Always loving you.

Your Loving,

Father.

xxxxxxxxxxxx

OPPOSITE: **Just before the Munich Crisis of 1938, Stella MacNally began to write to a young German sailor. When she received this letter from him, which included leading questions about defence matters, her father refused point blank to allow her to continue the correspondence.**

Because her father was the Canadian Pacific representative in Austria, Doreen King, a young English girl, was at school in Vienna from 1931 to 1934. She had many friends; one was Heinz Schramm-Schiesel, an Austrian boy of her own age. Both Doreen and Heinz

Tjüche, Kreis Norden
7/8/38.

Dear Stella!

You have made me a great joy by writing your letter. You are coming together, as if I have searched you. I everytime certenly have ... a corre-spondence w... ...

Before, I have ... ...
esting for th... ...
oldest brothe... ...
Iowa; and ... ... of that.
whole fa... ... natrose
this ce... ... te:
You as... ...
Freese is ...

seemed to realise that war was imminent. In August 1939 the King family was recalled to England. Before they left Doreen had received two letters from Heinz, by now at the Göppingen military training camp. The first letter sent wishes that he were with her so that he could see 'her divine face again'. The second, more serious in tone, thought that perhaps by the time she received the letter they would be enemies. He said that he would do his duty by his people, and hoped she would do the same by hers. He would do his duty so long as her 'wonderful eyes', which he always saw before him, did not tell him that their situation was impossible: 'I do not see why our people should not understand each other as well as we two do.' He closed with instructions as to how she should write to him without giving away his whereabouts.

Back in England, Doreen joined the WAAF and, being a fluent German-speaker, was posted to Y Force, a top secret organisation.

In 1941 Doreen met Tom Bathurst, with whom she exchanged hundreds of letters while he served with an Indian regiment in the Eighth Army in Egypt. A year after the end of the war a letter from Heinz Schramm-Schiesel arrived. 'You were right when you said that there would be war,' he started, 'and that England could never lose a war.' He told her of his anxiety for her when London was being bombed. 'To my great joy I never fought against English soldiers: you know how warm my feelings are towards your people.' They never met again.

Pilot Officer Victor Bagley was shot down over Holland on 13 March 1941. This tender letter is the last he sent his wife, to be opened if he never returned:

My Darling Baby,

Do you remember how little trivialities worried us a lot more than did seemingly important things, such as money and security? I realised then how important it was that we should always preserve the carefree happiness we have enjoyed so blissfully together. Now perhaps you have experienced a greater worry than all of these – you feel that your whole life has crumpled into the abyss of a fiendish nightmare, that even the dearest and kindest of your friends and own family cannot soothe your misery. My dearest one, I am writing this in perfect safety and yet I feel the very feelings you do now – as you realise that I have not returned. Dear sweet Jeanette, if God has spared me for you, as I know he will, then

I will come back to you. I am not asking you to be plucky or grimly patient – I know how you will behave and I know the torture you will suffer – I am sharing it with you – for my sake and for those that love you keep going and God will guard our love that is also his.

I have often wondered whether we should have met if little things had not occurred to throw us together – if they are responsible for our meeting then surely the same trivial occurrences can keep us together and prevent a material parting. If I am still on this earth I will pray for you as I have never prayed in Church or elsewhere, if I am not then I shall hear your prayers, my soul will always be with you as it is in life.

Soon trouble and strife will end on earth – sweet good things must blossom from the chaos and wickedness that caused so many to suffer. Love and unselfishness will be the foundations of a new order – clarity of mind and common sense will preserve it. The brief time we have known

Happier times – Pilot Officer Victor Bagley and his wife on their wedding day in the winter of 1940. They had been married for just four months when his aircraft was shot down over Holland.

When British servicemen sailed
for the Falklands in 1982 a new
generation of women endured the
anguish of quayside partings as
they waved their men off to war.

each other has for us been such a Utopia. We have between us known more of and been nearer to a perfect world than all the politicians and great statesmen, in their wildest dreams, have ever been. So God would have the world like us two – young and fresh and in perfect concord, with nothing but the responsibility of our own happiness to concern us.

If I could end my message to you in music I would, Baby – in my heart I hear the strains of a great melody that birds and trees know – I can see you too in a whirl of misty light, dancing as you would, towards me – and in your eyes, that love I have shared.

Soon you will be in my arms and we will dance together across galaxies and through the vast heavens as though they were just a ballroom.

Till then, my love, au revoir and God bless you.

Your loving husband,
Victor.

Eileen Kisby was sent a mother-of-pearl cross by her fiancé's commanding officer with a letter telling her he had been killed:

I will always remember it. We said Goodbye on Groombridge Station here in Kent not far from where I live now, I can still hear him saying I will be back. I did not have a ring but I gave him one before he left. A letter came and a beautiful Mother of Pearl Cross inside was sent to me by his Colonel to say he had been killed. I was so young I could not believe it, that was before I joined the ATS. I had waited to hear from him. When the letter came I was thrilled, what would I read, but I soon found out. He was so young.

When things did go wrong, someone had to pass the bad news on to the bereaved, a task which Margaret Smee found harrowing in the extreme:

The worst thing I ever had to do in the WRNS was to tell one of my girls that her husband had been killed. Just over three weeks earlier, we had happily attended her wedding to a young coastal forces officer we all knew well, as they met when he had been brought to our Christmas party. She came back after her honeymoon and went on duty in the tower. Bill went down to Appledore to collect a new MTB. While on board, a machine gun was accidentally triggered off and the phone call came through that he was dead. By this time, we had a new watchroom and tower about a quarter of a mile away, so I had to send someone to take her place, something quite unheard of. As soon as she got to the door she said, 'Is Bill dead?' I had no need to tell her.

Her mates comforted her as best they could and were quite marvellous. In fact there was very little of the bitchiness one might expect, with a

lot of young women flung together willy-nilly. On the whole they were an extraordinarily nice bunch of people.

Farewell heart's darling.
Embarkation leave, brief honeymoon.
The still of the night
Whispered your love for me.

In the still of the night
Breast to breast urged
Interposed the Creator divine
Bestowing His gift, our child.

Daybreak.

Evening and blackout.
Au revoir dear love.
In the dark depths of nightfall,
Torpedo and heartache.

Frank Macé

A gold locket containing a lock of hair and a photograph of Captain H C Blyde, worn by his wife throughout the First World War.

A young submariner, Ivor Gwyn Williams, sent the following letter to his sweetheart, to be opened in the event of his death. HM Submarine *Usk* was lost off Cape Bon in 1941. Gwyn's sister Myra still remembers her brother and his fellow sailors every day. Particularly touching is his hope that Betty will eventually have a happy marriage.

I.G. Williams
Submarine Usk.
18.4.41.
Dearest Betty,

Betty, my darling, I think that you won't mind me calling you that for the last time, as I expect by now my sister has informed you that I have died in fighting for our and other countries, but I may say, darling, that my last thoughts were of my family and you, and I love you while there is a breath in my body.

I take this the last opportunity of wishing you the happiest married life which it is possible for two people to have. And only wish that it was I. Also give my wishes for a happy and long life to your Mother, Father and all your friends and Relations, and with these few last words I close, wishing you all the very best.

Your most Loving Friend,
Gwyn.

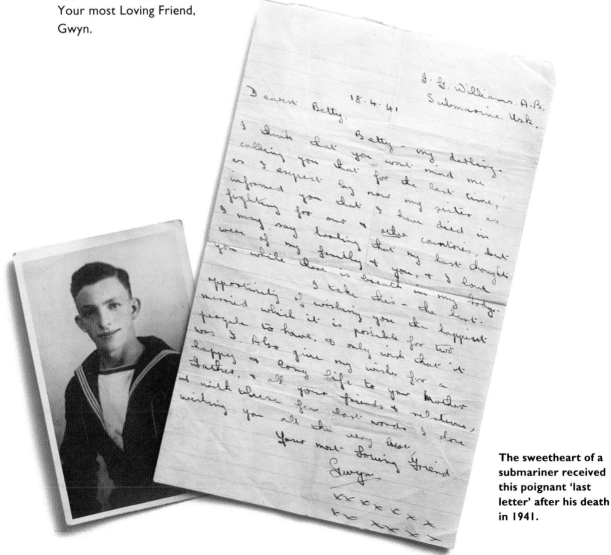

The sweetheart of a submariner received this poignant 'last letter' after his death in 1941.

Requiem for a Wren
(My Sweetheart killed in the Blitz on Liverpool in '40s)

Come back my love-one! My dear love returning
Love stands eternal, tho' youth may be fleeting.
Come in the Summer when Skye's Hills are purple,
Sweet with the heather the wanton bees fumble,
Pure as Zephyr from Sound of Sleat blowing.

Come in the Autumn! when Arctic Terns slender
Diving and gliding; those skimming Sea Swallows
Sewing together – invisible stitches
Cobbling shadows to dappled jade sunshine.
All this you loved, when we loved together.

Can you not hear them, the Razor Bills crying?
Guillemots perched on the cliff-top high ledges.
Black silhouetted and steep rears the coastline,
Frayed like a fjord and icy the ocean.
Fiercely the surf breaks o'er rocks in the channel.

Here like the rocks with the foam crashing over,
Throwing up curtains of spray in a rainbow.
Charybdis lurking where tide race runs narrow,
Pulling and sucking our boat in its whirlpool,
Can you not feel it, the shuddering rudder,
Can't you remember our past love together?

Call to me softly thro' Winter Winds wailing,
Even now gales pile-up walls of wild water,
Driving our battleship, bucking and slewing,
Decks stiff with ice, whilst the scupper's awash.
Will you be waiting when we reach safe harbour?

Perhaps you'll return when the lilac's in blossom?
Whilst in our rock pool the young seals are playing.
Plunging and screaming the hoards of gulls squabble,
Feeding on fresh fry, forced up to the surface,
Driven by shoals of blue mackerel, beneath.

Draw near, my love, in the quiet of evening,
Golden and pink as the heavens are fading,

OPPOSITE: **Gordon Charkin's Wren sweetheart, Betty, was killed during a German bombing raid on Liverpool.**

Leaving our world goes the sun at his setting,
Blood red his trail to the West at his passing,
Dark grey those streamers of cloud 'gainst the sunset.

Listen, my love, to the desolate music!
Haunting the calls of the Snow Geese and Greylags,
Flying in 'V'-form towards the last sunlight
Beating black wings standing bold 'gainst the sunset.
So comes the night with my loneliness bitter.

Gordon P. Charkin (unpublished)
1943

These verses were written on the destroyer HMS *Calpe* on an Arctic convoy to Murmansk. The original copy was destroyed by sea water.

Sam Curtis and Fred Barham both joined up as soon as war was declared in 1914. Before they left for France, Sam married Fred's sister, Louisa. As soon as the wedding service was over, Sam had to pack his kit-bag and go. After a year he was granted leave, but as he stood up to clamber out of his trench he was shot by a German sniper and died in Fred's arms. Fred served three more years, but died after both his legs were amputated. 'Louie' never remarried and went to live with her parents. Her pension was five shillings a week, later increased to seven shillings and sixpence. Among Fred's belongings which were returned to the family when he died was a photograph of Louie with a message written on the back.

8.7.16.
Dear Louie,
    If I should not see you again this side, shall meet you up higher.
    Sam and I shall be waiting for you. I wish you God speed. Keep smiling, am feeling merry and bright.
        Fondest love,
        Fred.

The sense of absolute desolation experienced by a war widow comes over very strongly in this moving account by Mrs Eckersley. It is transcribed from a sound recording and you can almost hear her voice when you read the words. The scene she describes of

Louisa Barham married Sam Curtis in 1914 on the day he left for France. He was killed a year later without their having seen each other again.

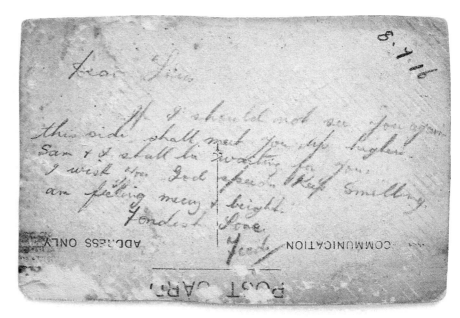

An American soldier returning from the Gulf War in March 1991 receives an ecstatic welcome from his wife.

Vesta Tilley's recruitment campaign was accurately invoked by Maggie Smith in the film *Oh What a Lovely War!* The 'he' she refers to is of course her husband:

He was a beautiful man and we worked together and we paid for our home together and we was extremely happy – no one was happier and I was very, very proud of him, especially with him being a member of the St Crosses' Church and then the war started and he didn't have any need to go to the war really – he had no need to go to the war because his job was painting cars, I believe. Anyway he was very patriotic, that was by the way – we go to the Palace and we see the show at the Palace and during the interval they had this recruiting campaign. Vesta Tilley was there and all the band on the stage – recruiting officers with the sashes and what have you – and she came out into the audience, walked all down – either sides – the men was getting up – out of their seats following her. She also had a big Union Jack wrapped round her and she introduced that song 'We don't want to lose you but we think you ought to go' – and we were sat at the front and she walked down and she hesitated a bit and she put her hand on my husband's shoulder and – all of it – all the place was full of the boys following her down and they couldn't really get on the stage – not all of them couldn't and he was with one of them and he got up and he went with her. And then he came home – we came home that night and I was terribly upset and I said I didn't want him to go and be a soldier – because I didn't want to lose him – I didn't want him to go at all, but he said, 'We have to go.' He said, 'There has to be men to go and fight for the women' – otherwise, he said, where should we be? And he eventually persuaded

OPPOSITE: **On her nationwide recruiting campaigns the actress Vesta Tilley convinced many men of their duty to serve their country.**

PHILCO SERIES 2062 D.   MISS VESTA TILLEY.

A perspex brooch with photographs of an airman and his girlfriend on either side of the pendant. The perspex from which it was made came from a Wellington bomber damaged during the first 'thousand bomber' raid on Germany in May 1942.

OPPOSITE: This traditional good-luck horseshoe was given to WAAF bride Olive New on her wedding day in 1944.

me that it was all for the best.

During the time that he was away I was very lonely – I did not make friends very easily and I – all – all the thoughts I had was for my husband.

Times was very, very hard and I only had 12/6 a week and therefore I could not go out and spend like anyone else and I used to sit at night and try to do a bit of reading or a bit of sewing with my hands to pass the time away but it was very, very hard and sometimes I would wonder – wonder what he was doing and if he was thinking about me and wondering how he was going on – when I should see him again – and all things like that.

So after I found that it was officially known he had been killed, I used to pass my time away trying to make little baby clothes for my baby – and eventually the baby came to be born. It was born at home, but I don't remember it being born at all. I had a very bad time – I had two doctors and I don't remember the baby being born – and I felt I didn't want to live – I'd no wish to live at all because the world had come to an end then for me because I'd lost all that I'd loved.

— 6 —
WEDDINGS

'Yours to the end of life's story'

I do not ask for wines
In never-ending store;
I do not seek renown
For fame can be a bore.
My choice is not for riches
For there's treachery in gold.
Nor do I seek a pardon
From ever growing old.
My choice would be quite simple
As common as a tree –
All I want is just a home
A home for you and me.

Sergeant Cy Pattengill – *Greatest Good*

OPPOSITE: **Ray and Olive New on their wedding day in 1944. Olive was the first wearer of the 'Roosevelt Dress' donated by the wife of the US President for the use of British servicewomen whose choice of gowns was restricted by clothes rationing and other shortages.**

Wartime clothes rationing made it extremely difficult for a bride to look glamorous on her wedding day. Clothing was 'on coupons' and material was 'under the counter'. Second Lieutenant Raymond New, Royal Artillery, and his bride-to-be, WAAF Olive Crofts, decided just before the D-Day landings to bring their wedding day forward. They suddenly feared that they might be saying goodbye for ever and they wanted to be married to each other. They saw the padre and were given a date for five days away. No time to read the banns, and Olive planned to borrow a dress from a friend's sister. Her WAAF officer, however, had another idea. Mrs Eleanor Roosevelt, wife of the US president, had banded together with leading society ladies in America to donate beautiful, lavish wedding dresses for British service brides to wear. 'The Roosevelt Dress' had been given to Maintenance Command and its units – the cost to the bride was just ten shillings for the cleaning bill after the ceremony. Olive New remembers . . .

. . . a gorgeous creation in heavy embossed cream brocade, Tudor in style, with long pointed sleeves, gathered waist falling into a four-yard circular train and topped with a long silk veil. Juliet cap and garland and flowers. With it I was to carry a bouquet of lilies of the valley, violas and stocks – all that was available at the time – it was beautiful!

The dress came via lorry from Andover to Warminster and friends provided bridesmaids' dresses from Liverpool and Frome. Somehow head-dresses and accessories were found. Olive bought her own wedding ring and ordered cars. The RAF personnel rallied round, providing beds for Raymond and for Olive's father, a Chief Petty Officer RN. Her adjutant offered to be best man, and another officer played the organ. The signals section made up buttonholes and the bridesmaids' bouquets; Olive's best friend, a hairdresser in civilian life, washed and set several sets of hair, and her own, between transmitting and receiving teleprinted messages in the early hours of the morning. The reception was held in the NAAFI, and food was provided by the American army; hearing of the Roosevelt dress connection they supplied a huge feast and a two-tiered wedding cake. The guard of honour outside the church were Olive's WAAF friends:

What a wedding – all arranged in just five days. For a day the war really stood still.

Vera married Fred Kelly in a dress provided by Dame Barbara Cartland, then a commander in the ATS. Barbara Cartland was determined to help ATS and other service brides marry in the gown of their dreams. She bought over 120 dresses which could be used by any servicewoman for £1.

Not everyone was lucky enough to borrow a beautiful dress for the wedding. Jean Kent was a hugely popular stage and screen star in the 1930s and '40s. This letter was written in response to a request to borrow one of her film costumes.

Gainsborough Studios
Lime Grove, London W.12.
Dear Lt Brown,

Thank you for your letter. I am afraid I cannot help you personally in regard to a wedding dress because I have to use mine frequently for personal appearances. If, however, you wrote to Mr Bohar at Gainsborough Studios, he may be able to help as dresses are loaned out in special circumstances. Give him full details of measurements, &c.

Sorry I cannot be more helpful, but I only have the same coupon allowance as everybody else.

All good wishes,
Yours sincerely,
Jean Kent.

But ingenuity knew no bounds. Dresses were made from curtains and tablecloths, and silk from parachutes was widely used if it was white: some parachutes, however, were orange. Poppy Hambly and her sister were presented with a delightful gift from two airmen they were dating:

When they opened a kit-bag they had brought with them, out fell a parachute. It must have been against regulations, of course, but we had heard of other people who had been given parts of one, and now we had a whole one to ourselves. It was cut into sections because it was so large to handle, and in the weeks that followed we all had new orange silk undies. I took some to the girls at work, and still there was more left over.

Maureen Bolster, writing to her fiancé, Eric Wells, provides a reminder that material was not the only thing in short supply in the war years.

ENSA artiste Jean Neville had her wedding dress made from the softly flowing silk salvaged from a parachute.

Flight Lieutenant Derek Read and his fiancée, Julie, had only twenty-four hours in which to arrange their wedding at his German base before he flew off to the Gulf in January 1991.

Hair-grips, tape, sewing materials and needles have to be scrounged. The one thing the shops do seem full of is toothpaste. Dress material is becoming poor, lingerie's an enormous price. One can buy lipstick fairly easily but handcream and other creams are rare. Perfume is unobtainable apart from the 5 guinea per tiny bottle variety that no one can afford and is probably black market anyway. Still, one doesn't mind. They are such very minor details after all.

Julie and Derek Read were married on the day Derek was posted to the Gulf: 24 January 1991. Their wedding was arranged in approximately twenty-four hours when they realised that they would have to cancel their plans to marry in March. No members of their families could be present, but they were overwhelmed by the kindness of the people around. Julie had only been working at RAF Laarbruch for two weeks as a teacher, and had just one close friend, who was her bridesmaid. The flowers came from the local supermarket. Julie's wedding dress was in the process of being made in Scotland, so she wore a dress of dark green velvet she had worn as a bridesmaid at her sister's wedding. That night, her wedding night, she watched a Hercules aircraft taking her husband off to war, from which he luckily returned.

Second Lieutenant HCL Heywood, serving with the 6th Manchesters in Egypt in 1915, was one of three guests at a hastily arranged marriage: the battalion had learnt on 29 April that they were to leave Egypt for Gallipoli at short notice. On 1 May he wrote:

OPPOSITE: Flight Lieutenant Derek Read pictured in the Gulf, with (INSET) a Valentine card he sent to his wife Julie in February 1991. The card was inscribed: 'Sorry for the naff design – it was so bad I just had to have it.'

Saturday was a day of hustle at first, and slackness afterwards. We had a kit inspection in the morning, puzzled ourselves to death finding out how many bootlaces one's platoon wanted; or how many identity discs were missing; or if the pay books were filled up right. At last it was done, and then I hustled down to Cairo to attend the wedding of one of our officers. The ceremony took place at the Chapel at Kasr-el-nil, and the congregation numbered five; the two parties interested, a Russian girl of 23 who was the bride's friend (the bride was French and spoke English badly), Tommy

OPERATION
DESERT
SHIELD

Mills, and myself. It was weird in the extreme.

Arrived back to the mess about 5 p.m. and was greeted with the news that we were moving Sunday night.

The next day they packed and that evening set off for Gallipoli.

A month earlier, Commander GC Dickens RN recorded in his diary another wedding – his own. He was in command of the destroyer HMS *Harpy* in the Mediterranean and home waters. Later he became an admiral and was knighted. In his diary, as in Lieutenant Heywood's, one has a glimpse of the difficulties experienced when trying to make any personal plans – Commander Dickens was despatched to the Dardanelles a fortnight after he wrote the first entry quoted here:

26th March 1915. Suddenly told we (i.e. the 8 boats of 'Beagle' class sent home from the Mediterranean in November) were to go back to the Mediterranean. Boats were going in pairs and we will have to go any moment. What price the wedding?

27th. Pearl arrived in Portsmouth in answer to my wire. Find now, *Harpy* will sail with *Savage* in last pair. Our last transport that night. She went to Dieppe via Beachy Head. We averaged over the ground from the Nab to B. Head 6.2 knots!

28th. Arrived back in Portsmouth. 2.30 p.m! How I cursed. That was the worst transport trip we'd ever done. Pearl and I went up to town.

29th March. We were married in the Oratory at 2.30 p.m. Father Crewes officiated. I'll try to put down the names of people who came – at very short notice. Not attempting to write any details about the wedding or the honeymoon. They would be rather out of place in this record of war.

The two families of in-laws, of course, C. Georgy, Dusa, Nab, G. Bulley, Nansy our old nurse, Jane, Frida, Fal. von Wech, Gertie Orr Ewing and Archie, Daisy Barry, Cara, Lady Allchin, Mrs Pope and Ethel Bush, Marinetta Roche and Felicie, Major Thomas, the Gaelix; went off to the Metropole at Folkestone. Couldn't have chosen better. Splendid weather most of the time. Stayed there from Monday to Saturday, then town, put up two nights at an awful spot – the Strand Palace Hotel. Then on to Lyndhurst, 'The Crown'. Ripping, etc. etc. etc. While at Folkestone ran over to Hythe to say goodbye to the Mater, Guv, Ceddy and Bobs.

Arrived at Queen's Hotel Southsea Frid. 9th. So we managed to get 10 days' honeymoon after all instead of, as we thought, a few hours.

10th April. Said goodbye, and sailed for Dardanelles.

In 1930, Admiral Sir Richard Phillimore observed, rather crustily, in a draft covering four pages:

A marriage allowance for officers is very undesirable. To begin with it should be a matter of pure indifference to the Higher Authorities of a Fighting Service whether an officer is married or not, so long as he is efficient . . . A naval officer's interest should be centred in the service and most of us have had occasion to notice the disturbing effect of a wife's presence on the Station in the case of Young Officers.

He continues sternly in this vein, but surely there is a glimmer of a twinkle in his eye when he returns to the subject of money:

Vernon and Doris Browne's photograph album is the story of 'one happy year, 43–44'. It covers their meeting, courtship and marriage – Vernon sent a cutting of Patience Strong's verses with every letter he wrote to Doris. Patience Strong's poetry was hugely popular and her sentiments sustained many women (and men) through the war years and afterwards.

Our second leave together . . . December 13th. – 23rd.

Taking a stroll at Torquay.

— The Tapestry of Time —

Life works out a pattern on the tapestry of Time. The threads of hope, of love and grief, of fear and faith sublime—of happiness and bitterness, of joy and misery—are stitched into the great design of human destiny. Within so vast a frame, our tiny patch we cannot see. Too close we stand to trace the pattern on the tapestry. . . . But someday, looking from afar, perhaps we shall behold—Our little bit of the design; our own small thread of gold. PATIENCE STRONG.

"A dink, . . . a dink - a - do."

. . . . . with Mrs Kirby at Paignton.

... judging from the number of young married Officers who own motor cars, there do not appear to be widespread pecuniary difficulties to prevent these young marriages, even in the absence of a marriage allowance.

Commanding officers in all the services had to be deferred to where marriage was concerned. Permission had to be sought and approval given. Sergeant Earl Adkins, serving with the US Army, 'having read and thoroughly understood' the file on 'Overseas

Eighteen-year-old Dorothy Chamberlin from Doncaster had to sign a formal Declaration to Marry letter before she was allowed to wed her GI fiancé, Earl Adkins. Her parents also had to write to his commanding officer giving their consent to the marriage.

6 Grove Vale,
Wheatley Hills,
Doncaster, England.

SUBJECT: Declaration to Marry.

TO : Commanding Officer, 369th Fighter Squadron, 359th Fighter Group, APO 557, U.S. Army.

Under the provisions of Circular 41, Headquarters European Theatre of Operations, dated 17 April 1944, which I have read and thoroughly understand, the following is submitted:

a. Name: Dorothy M. Chamberlin   Age: 18

b. Address: 6 Grove Vale, Wheatley Hills, Doncaster, England

c. I wish to marry Sgt Earl D. Adkins.   ASN: 18050423

d. I am not married at this time.

e. I understand that, when married, my intended husband will not be permitted any special privileges or living arrangements different from those of unmarried members of the command of which he is a member.

f. I understand that marriage to a citizen of the United States does not confer United States citizenship on an alien, under existing law, although it does facilitate the alien's entry into the United States and naturalization after taking up residence there.

g. I understand that I will not be entitled to any privileges including commissary, post exchange, government quarters, medical or dental services.

h. I understand that I will be entitled to such allowances, allotments, insurance and other benefits as authorized by law upon completion of marriage.

D. M. Chamberlin.
(Signature)

Marriages of Military Personnel', sent in a letter to the commanding officer of the 369th Fighter Squadron, stationed in England in 1945. He enclosed his fiancée Dorothy Chamberlin's Declaration to Marry letter, in which she confirmed her understanding of what privileges she would and would not have. She would not become an American citizen, they would not be permitted any special privileges or living arrangements, nor medical, dental, post exchange, government quarters or commissary services. She would be entitled to 'such allowances, allotments and insurance as authorised by law'. She also enclosed her parents' written consent.

Permission was granted after 'investigation reveals that both parties are eligible to marry, and that such marriage will not bring discredit to the Military Service'.

Despite this fairly daunting procedure, tens of thousands of girls married servicemen from Allied or Dominion countries. Leaving your own country to live permanently in another is at any time a tremendous upheaval, but in wartime there were extra stresses to consider. Quite often the marriage would have been arranged rapidly, emotional hearts ruling over sober heads, and the heat of the moment sometimes cooled into disillusionment and homesickness. For some there were unromantic shocks awaiting them when they discovered that the realities of their new homeland didn't match up to their husbands' promises. Some became desperately lonely, some found they were not welcome.

Ida Faulkner travelled to New Zealand on the *Ionic* at the end of the First World War; her husband Bert was in the ship's hospital and she visited him every afternoon. Despite seasickness and anxiety, she was full of optimism about her life so far from home:

> The Alphabet by Ida Faulkner
>
> A   is for ARMY of which we are fond
> B   is for BRIDES both brunette and blonde
> C   is for COURAGE they had lots
> D   is for DISTANCE we covered by knots
> E   is for ENDEAVOUR to give of our best
> F   is for FORTITUDE put to the test
> G   is for GIRLS tall, short, thin and fat
> H   is for HONEY we were called that
> I   is for IONIC a wonderful ship
> J   is for JOURNEY a marvellous trip

K	is for	KINDRED we'll see never more
L	is for	LONGING to land on the shore
M	is for	MOTHERS wherever they dwell
N	is for	NOBLE hearts who wished us well
O	is for	OCEAN so wide and so blue
P	is for	PATER so trusting and true
Q	is for	QUARRELS we hope we have none
R	is for	ROMANCE a duty well done
S	is for	SHAW SAVILL who owned our good ship
T	is for	TRAVELLERS so young and so fit
U	is for	UNIFORMS khaki and blue
V	is for	VICTORY it's coming soon
W	is for	WHO had the stout heart
X	is for	KISSING we've done lots of that
Y	is for	YOUTH we've left behind us
Z	is for	ZEALAND who love us they must.

The corsage worn by Daisy Durtnall when she married Joseph Cooper in Hammersmith, London, on 24 July 1918, shown here with congratulatory telegrams and a silver shoe from their wedding cake.

At the same time a London-born bride of an Australian serviceman remembers a hostile reception:

There was a lot of ill feeling at the time, the chief sentiment being that these 'fast' English girls (definitely not ladies!) had whisked away innocent Australian soldiers to the altar. The debate went on for many months in the Melbourne *Truth* newspaper, a weekly tabloid:

November 1919.

Sir – In reply to 'Digger's' dismal display in *Truth* – he isn't much credit to his birthplace and breeding if he thinks they can raise a better sample of a woman in England than in the country of his birth. My brother brought back an English bride. Before they landed, she was lauded up the skies as being beautiful, accomplished, helpful and brilliant, so we looked forward to seeing something that wouldn't be a disgrace to the family; but instead of that we found an ugly, brown-necked, red-complexioned, lazy hussy who had not a good word to say about anyone or anything in this country; found fault with all and sundry, was a spendthrift and to boot was *one of the biggest liars* we ever met.

Speaking personally it was a sorry day for me when an imported minx landed in our family. England contains good girls, same as any other country; but they have not got a monopoly of all of them, thank goodness; and anyway their social and factory life tends to produce, I should imagine, a lower type than our own sunny land.

Yours etc.,
'LOCAL GOODS'

After the Second World War some 60,000 GI brides sailed to the USA. One who didn't was Stella, Mrs Theodore H. Soehle. Stella had met Private 'Ted' Soehle in Somerset before he was sent to France in 1944. Just before he left, they discovered that Stella was expecting his baby and he arranged to get back to England for five days in the autumn to marry her, borrowing money from his friends for their brief honeymoon. On 8 December he wrote from France:

It feels fine to me to be married, how does it feel to you? I sure hated to leave you, darling, but the way I look at it, we were lucky to even be together at all. They were five days I'll never forget, but there'll be a lot more after the war is over. It is just three years today since Pearl Harbor, but it really shouldn't be much longer now. Will have to stop now, darling, please write as often as you can.
    All my love,
    Your husband, Ted.

A month later, he wrote anxiously:

Dearest Stella,
    Received your 2nd letter today. What has been the trouble? Surely you can average better than two letters a month if you try. I thought you had been bombed out or something . . . Does the doctor still think that it will be April? I'll be glad when it is over and I guess you will too. Wish I could be there with you . . . Take good care of yourself, Stella, and *please* write more often so I won't worry any more than I do. See you soon.
    All my love,
    Ted.

Jan 12th 45.
    It really is a hell of a married life we are having isn't it, hon? We will have an awful lot to make up for after this thing is over. I couldn't love you more if I were twins, darling. I miss you more every day.
    You should get your first check very soon if you haven't gotten it already. It should be for two months of $100.00 equal to 22 pounds 10 shillings. Take good care of yourself for me, darling, until I can take care of you myself.
    Love, Ted.
Write more often *please*.

Ted had arranged that after the first lump sum, fifty dollars would be paid to her on the first of every month:

The wedding of Dorothy Alice Marshall and Sydney Hall in 1918 had to be brought forward as Sydney's ship was suddenly 'under orders'. The exquisitely delicate beaded lace dress (OPPOSITE) was still at the dressmaker's and the bridesmaid was on holiday – but the dress was finished in the small hours and a substitute bridesmaid found. Sydney and Dorothy snatched a brief two-day honeymoon before he rejoined his ship.

It won't leave me enough to pay for my laundry, but I'm not complaining about it.

By March he found that his meagre pay packet wouldn't cover all his outgoings:

Since they took the allotments out of my pay I haven't been able to get any money ahead – what with paying the boys back for my honeymoon trip and my rations I'm always broke. Will you please send me fifty dollars as soon as possible so I can get out of debt . . . be sure and send me a copy of the birth certificate as soon as you can. It will mean thirty more dollars every month to us. I guess it won't be long now until the little sprout gets here, will it? I guess you are as big as a house now. Hope you don't lose that million dollar figure. I want to gaze at that plenty after the war is won. It seems like you're on my mind all the time. I know there is no way I could help but I sure would like to be there for the arrival of the new *Yank*.

April 22nd, 45.
  Dearest Stella, I suppose this letter will find you a mother. How does it feel to be a parent? Did you have a very hard time, honey? I certainly hope not – I'm with the Ninth Army now . . .

Same letter, completed on 6 May:

The Germans are surrendering so fast we are up almost 24 hours a day. The end is really in sight now, honey. Received your letter today. Words can't express my feelings, darling. How are you feeling, all right? I wish I could have been there . . . By the way, you didn't tell me the baby's name.

June 3rd.
  I can see you don't intend to write so will make this last attempt.

August 30th, 1945.
Marseille,
France.
Dearest Stella,
  Well, darling, I don't know what to think about you. I haven't had a word for three months now. Down in your heart do you really think you're being fair? Where you are concerned at least I think I have done my share. I was man enough to go to a lot of trouble and expense to come all the way from France to London to marry you. I certainly didn't have to do that if I didn't want to. All I ask is that you be decent enough to let me know what you want to do. I don't believe that is asking too much. I don't imagine you care to go to the States with me and live, if not what

do you want to do? Are you going to get a divorce? I could've had a furlough to England about a month ago, but the way you are carrying on I turned it down. I wasn't sure I'd be welcome.

I'm to leave for home, if nothing happens, in a few days. The plans are now we are to fly. Please write soon and let me know what your plans are, that's all I ask of you and it isn't much. I'll admit I wasn't much of a husband but I didn't have much chance to be one either.

All my love,

Ted.

That was the last letter poor Ted sent.

For every marriage that foundered, there were many that were triumphantly happy and enduring. Fred Tustin's wedding to Marguerite nearly didn't take place:

During the Liberation of Brussels our Unit received help from the Resistance movement. One beautiful girl, who spoke perfect English, told us her English mother was a nurse in Leicester during the 1914–18 war,

Lilian and Ramsay Bader cutting a celebratory cake in his parents' garden a few days after their wedding in 1943. They met while he was in the army and she was serving in the WAAF.

175

had nursed a Belgian soldier wounded at Ypres and convalescing in Leicester. They married and the girl went to Belgium aged two years. At the outbreak of the 1939 war, they all joined the Resistance.

At one period nearing the end of the war, our CO wanted an interpreter who spoke English, German, French and Flemish. We advised him to contact the Resistance in Brussels.

Along came this beautiful girl and was duly installed in her own office next to the colonel. I was jokingly called 'the Unit Casanova' and bets were laid that I could date this lovely girl. One day in the Company Stores I saw her leaning on the counter reading an English newspaper. With the bets in mind I blurted out, 'Would you have a drink with me one day.' Giving me that lovely smile she said, 'I can't have you losing your bet.' I blushed like a beetroot.

As time went by we became deeply attached. It worried me, as my nickname was 'Love 'em and leave 'em'. This girl I loved and respected. My mother had died when I was 2 years old – I was in and out of children's homes, knowing no loving home life: in fact, a Rough Diamond.

I said to Marguerite one day, 'I am getting very fond of you but life with me for any girl would be no fun, having no future and nothing to offer. It is best we part before we get too deeply attached.' I asked my CO for a posting and set off in a jeep.

After about 2 hours I said to myself, 'Why? You love the girl.' I turned round and headed back to Brussels. I arrived at her parents' house at about 4 a.m. and rang the bell. Her father's head appeared at his bedroom window. 'Thought you'd left,' he said. Then the light came on downstairs and the front door opened. It was Marguerite and I could see she had been crying. I said, 'I have nothing to offer you. Will you marry me?' We fell into each other's arms.

In due course the Army Chaplain from Christchurch, Brussels, came to see us and we chose a date. I was reinstated into my Unit: we all had a grand celebration the night before the wedding. We crawled into bed at about 3 a.m., to be woken again by church bells ringing all over Belgium. I thought, surely the Army hasn't laid this on specially? But we soon found out. It was VJ Day: we were married on VJ Day, August 15th 1945. What a day to remember!

Late in 1940 John Lockwood, a young pilot with No. 1 Squadron, Royal Australian Air Force, was stationed at Sembawang in Malaya. There he met Betty, daughter

Australian pilot John Lockwood married his English sweetheart Betty Percy in Singapore in January 1942 while the Japanese air attacks were at their height.

of an English civil engineer, Lieutenant-Colonel Percy. They became unofficially engaged; later No.1 Squadron was moved north to Kota Bharu in 1941. John had a nephew still at school in Australia, who idolised his dashing uncle. The boy's name was Bill, and Betty used to write him long letters. At the height of the Japanese air attacks in 1942, John Lockwood married Betty Percy. Two weeks later his squadron was withdrawn to Sumatra, and the young couple never saw each other again. In 1944 Betty wrote to Bill, then aged sixteen, telling of her wedding to 'Locky' and the withdrawal from Malaya:

You get a rather confused idea of war when it is actually in your garden, but you do realise the horror of it. The last few weeks in Malaya were lived at fever pitch, and even now I feel a bit vague about them, with little things standing out in my memory instead of the big things. One of the most vivid things is the memory of being held up at the level crossing one day when I was driving down to the medical depot. A long, long train was going through, with truckloads of wounded Indian soldiers; very few of them had had their wounds dressed, and it was rather horrible, but every one of them was smiling, and I didn't know whether I wanted to go all Victorian and weep or get up and cheer. The Indian fighting men are fine, and they did terrific work in Malaya, against the Japanese.

Betty Lockwood was widowed only a month after her marriage to 'Locky' in 1942.

The RAAF fought a very big action at Kota Bharu, and you can be very proud of them. Over here pilots and crews are rested after operations, and nursed up for the next one. At KB (and through the whole Malayan campaign) the same people took off every night, and patrolled every day. It must have been the most gruelling life for them, and I know how tired Locky was. Every one of them did it cheerfully and willingly. A good many of the fellows of the Squadron were lost; it got so that I was frightened to ask Locky how anyone was, in case his mouth tightened and he said, 'He bought it.'

KB fell very quickly, and those that could got out. Locky, I think, must have been one of the last people out, and he was chased down country by Japanese fighter planes. We had been trying to get in touch with him, and he with us, but there were no communications. Then he rang up one evening, and came over as soon as he could, tired and hungry, unshaven and with the filthiest clothes on. He sank a Japanese transport before he got away.

Life seemed to be one long take-off after that, any hour in the early morning. He used to spend all his spare time with us, and get back to the airfield when he was needed. As he used to have to get back so early in the morning, we couldn't call the servants to cook breakfast, so Daddy had a small electric cooker fitted up in the Chinese boy's servery (sort of butler's pantry), and I used to cook him lashings of eggs and bacon and coffee before driving him back to Sembawang. He never used to talk about himself, so I don't know a lot of what happened, but I do know that he did some very big things, and he must have needed a lot of courage. Perhaps he knew that it would have worried me if he'd talked about the raids he'd been on, or perhaps he just wanted to forget them. I don't know, and I didn't ask him any questions. Other people in his squadron used to tell me things about him, otherwise I'd never had known anything.

On one raid he had a shrapnel splinter in his back, and went into hospital to have it removed. He went in on Monday morning, I think, and on Friday evening he rang me up and said he'd persuaded them to turn him loose, and he had two days' sick leave. He had got hold of the RAAF padre, and he said we had better get married the next afternoon. On Saturday morning we tore into Singapore and wangled a special licence out of the Archdeacon in the midst of one of the worst air raids I've ever known in my life. We couldn't get a wedding ring because all the shops had closed for the duration, and I was mad because I couldn't get a new dress. We borrowed Mummy's wedding ring, but when we got to the church we hadn't got a Best Man. Daddy lay low until one of his assistant engineers turned up to join the party, then he got hold of him and told him he was about to be a Best Man.

Jimmy Emerton gave us an iced Christmas cake to use as a wedding cake, and we managed to get some champagne from the Sultan's Club. Mummy cut the 'Christmas greetings' off the cake. Locky was still unwell, and could hardly stand up all the time we were being married, but he went back on duty early Monday morning, after we had spent the rest of Saturday and all Sunday dodging bombs and splinters. We spent Sunday morning sitting on the floor of the bar in the Tanglin Club, drinking vast quantities of tomato juice. We found the club had been turned into a first-aid station, and in any case was deserted – but the bar was open, so we simply went in and made ourselves at home.

Things got more and more confused after that; people were pouring down country, getting away from the advancing Japanese. Locky's squadron was flying sortie after sortie, and our army was being cut to pieces. When the Japanese were five or six miles up the road from us in Johore Bahru we had to move out. Locky was waiting for orders to proceed to Sumatra and wanted us to leave. His orders came through, but he remained behind after the rest of the squadron had gone, until the morning we sailed.

OPPOSITE: It seemed that Lance-Corporal Lancaster might have to delay his wedding: on the day he was expected home, on the eve of his wedding day, he found himself still in Calais with 7,000 other soldiers from the British Liberation Army unable to board their ships because of a gale in the Channel. Lancaster had reckoned without his future mother-in-law, Mrs Hannay. She telephoned the War Office, who promised to help. Lance-Corporal Lancaster was hustled on to the first ship and met by a loudspeaker announcer calling his name; two army officers bundled him on to a London train minutes before it pulled out and at Victoria the bemused soldier was rushed from the train and thrust into a taxi ahead of a long queue. His kit-bag was flung in after him by a smiling Irish sergeant, and the taxi hurtled him to his home just in time to clean up, dress and bolt for the church. The *Evening News* had taken the precaution of putting their reporter with him in the cab. Sharing the front page was the announcement that the ban on fraternisation between Allied soldiers and German girls had been lifted.

The Evening News

NO. 19,803   LONDON, SATURDAY, JULY 21, 1945   ONE PENNY

LATE EXTRA

LS "DEAR DESERT RATS"

Unsurpassed: May Your Glory Ever Shine'

SMILES BETWEEN FRATERNISERS. Allied soldiers and German girls keep company after the ban had been lifted. Photograph taken in the Berlin district.

BIG 3 : 'MUCH ALREADY DONE'

—Official

PREMIER FLYING HOME FOR RESULTS DAY

First concrete statement since the Big Three conference started, issued in Potsdam to-day, said : " The conference is going ahead and much serious business, has been done."

" Evening News " Political Correspondent

MR. CHURCHILL will fly home next week, as planned, so that he can be in London on Thursday when the results of the general election are announced.

Although doubts have been expressed whether he would, after all, make the journey, I understand that nothing has arisen to cause him to alter his plan to spend a day or so over here during the Potsdam talks.

Attlee May Come Too

Mr. Attlee, leader of the Labour Party, may also return, but his intentions are not so well known.

By next Tuesday, much of the main conversations between the " Big Three " may have been completed. At some point whether

---

60 'Extras' Rush Londoners to the Seaside

" Evening News " Reporter

MORE than 60 special trains, each carrying up to a thousand passengers, led another great London holiday rush to the coast to-day—one of the biggest for six years.

Despite an unsettled week-end weather outlook thousands queued at the Main Line stations for the South-East coast and the Country.

Here are reports showing how London's near-record holiday crowds got away.

Paddington: Half-mile queue—one of the longest ever seen, and greater than last Saturday's, which G.W.R. officials thought a record. New method of marshalling waiting passengers outside the station resulted in big speed-up.

Most long-distance trains were duplicated.

Peak Period

Waterloo : Summer exodus appeared to be at its zenith, with normal services to the resorts doubled. Eighteen extra trains to Bournemouth, Portsmouth, Isle of Wight and the West Country.

Victoria : Forty specials and a 15-minute service to the Kent coast; all trains packed. Margate, Ramsgate, Broadstairs and Brighton the favourite destinations.

Liverpool-street : Relief trains to Yarmouth, Lowestoft and Cambridge area. All trains full but no one left behind.

King's Cross : Queues from 6 a.m. Seven relief trains, and more standing by.

Workers' Playtime

Euston and St. Pancras : Little queueing, thanks to 13 extra trains to Blackpool, North Wales, and the Lake District.

More than 15,000 Luton warworkers are taking their first peace-time holiday this week-end, when the two biggest weaponmaking factories close.

THE QUEEN MARY HERE TO-MORROW

CIVILIANS ON BOARD FOR THE FIRST TIME

" Evening News " Reporter

THE " Queen Mary " will revive pre-war glories with a distinguished passenger list when she anchors off Greenock from New York to-morrow.

She is expected to arrive about 1.30 p.m. Among her passengers—who include a large number of both troops and civilians —are Princess Juliana of Holland ; Mr. J. A. Rank, the film magnate ; Robert Montgomery, film star ; Viscountess Byng ; and Mr. George Thompson, American Labour leader.

MAKE WAY, PLEASE, FOR THE B.L.A. BRIDEGROOM

SEVEN THOUSAND soldiers from the B.L.A. were crowded into the transit camp at Calais early to-day waiting for the ships that were to carry them home across the Channel. Then a voice came over the camp loud-speaker.

" Calling Lance-Corporal J. Lancaster," said the voice. " Will Lance-Corporal J. Lancaster please report at once."

Corporal Lancaster stepped out from the seven thousand. He was hurried down to the harbour and thrust aboard the first ship to sail.

When he landed at Folkestone after a rough crossing he heard his name being shouted on the loud speakers as he came ashore.

Army officers met him as he reported, hurried him to the station and pushed him into a Londonbound train just as it was moving out.

The Front of the Queue

The same thing happened at Victoria Station. Corporal Lancaster was rushed from the train to a taxi. A long queue was waiting for taxis ; the corporal was given a place at the head of the queue ; and a smiling Irish sergeant flung the corporal's kitbag into the taxi as it drove off.

And the taxi sped off across London to Greenwood-avenue, Hackney, where the corporal lives. The time was 11 a.m. At midday Corporal Lancaster had a date at St. Bartholomew's Church, Dalston—a date with Miss Eileen Hannam.

He cleaned up after his journey, hurried through some breakfast, and hurried off to the church.

Miss Hannam sighed with relief to see him arrive. So did her mother.

The Wedding Hustle

It was Miss Hannay's mother who had contrived it.

The wedding had been fixed months ago. The guests had been invited, the bride had bought the frock ; everything had been arranged.

Then last night came news of the Channel gale and of the holdup of the leave ships.

Mrs. Hannam telephoned the War Office and asked them to help. Army Movement Control got busy at once. If Corporal Lancaster could be got home in time they said he would get home.

They kept their word.

" It was a near thing," said Corporal Lancaster to The Evening News reporter who accompanied him in his taxi ride from Victoria to-day. " I cannot thank the War Office enough : they gave me priority all the way."

Lance-Corporal J. Lancaster.

IN MEMORY OF AIRMAN SON

FORTUNE FOR NEPHEW WHO TAKES HIS NAME

" Evening News " Correspondent

ON April 7, 1940, Lanby Dixon, beloved airman son of Mr. Hugh Wainwright Dixon, of Falconer's House, St. James' Court, and Blackfriars House, New Bridge-street, lost his life in an air accident.

To-day, in his £43,554 will, Mr. Dixon expresses his greatest wish and desire that his nephew, Anthony Dixon Green, should take the place of his son and adopt the name of Dixon.

Mr. Anthony Green, now 19, and in the Army, is the son of Dr. J. D. Green of Bournemouth.

Mr. Hugh Dixon, who owned shares in L. S Dixon and Co. and the Hurcott Paper Mills, left threefourths of his shares to his nephew. Anthony Green provided he enters the family business of L. S. Dixon and Co.

A bequest of £1,000 is also made to the Air Ministry Welfare Department to endow a bed in

---

3 NATIONS FLY TO WAR CRIMES COURT

RUSSIANS WITHDRAW AT THE LAST MOMENT

Britain, U.S. and France left to-day by plane for Nuremburg to examine the facilities for the trial of the major European Axis war prisoners and to select a site for the first and main trial. They expect to return to-morrow.

At the last moment the Soviet delegation advised that circumstances had unexpectedly arisen which made it impossible for either of its two members to go.

The British representatives were: the Attorney-General (Sir David Maxwell Fyfe), Mr. G. D. Roberts, K.C., Major - General Lord Bridgeman, of the War Office, and

---

[left column]

CH

PS

Jack-
10,000
s and
parade
Berlin's

bulk of
Premier
British
ghway
t Rats,
laurels

e which
Berlin
leads
surpassed
f war,
ters of in
r, dressed
form of a
his base
who had
the Nar-
River Elbe
Charlot-
wake of
D-day
carrier's
gleaming
concealed
battles

here

every-
ands of
Desert
of the
ear of
Navy
men of

Cana-
part,
behind
ughter
the
litary
oreign

Field-
Gen-
Com-
band
ugh
rtant
rtant
Three
Eden,
Mr.

2,000,000 U.S. 'DEMOBS'

By Next June

Just before we left the docks Daddy and David managed to get down to say goodbye again, and while we were shouting over the side of the ship to them Locky flew over in his Hudson on his way out, and came down to dip his wings, the way he used to over our house in JB. (Once he dropped a letter in a cigarette tin in the middle of our tennis court, from an aircraft.) And that was the last we saw of them.

Betty's father and brother-in-law, David, became prisoners of war, but Locky was never accounted for. After completing several more missions, he was ordered on the morning of 14 February to take part in an attack on a Japanese convoy approaching Palembang. Five Hudsons were assigned, three RAF, two RAAF. Only one returned. Locky was last seen losing height, under attack from two enemy Zeros, with smoke pouring from one engine.

> Some day, when the war is over
> And the darkness silvers away,
> We two, rose-crowned, shall know again,
> The dawn of a happier day.

Tony Conquest

When Ken Eyre married his wife in 1943, the wedding photographs were taken using a colour film bought in New York, a rare luxury in those days. Ken's father-in-law was very interested in photography and was delighted with the film. The day of 13 October was dull and wet and if the neighbours hadn't rallied round with food coupons, there would have been a very real danger of a reception based around bread and treacle. But all went well and the happy couple posed in the drizzle in the back garden. Now came the snag: although Ken and his two new brothers-in-law were sailors and would all be visiting New York where the film could be processed, his father-in-law refused to part with it, maintaining that their ships might be torpedoed and the treasured film lost. Time passed, the war ended and still they hadn't seen the wedding pictures. Eventually, aged eighty-nine, Ken's father-in-law died and the still unprocessed film came into Ken's possession. He

OPPOSITE: **GI Joe Fournier married Jean Ellerby, an English girl, on 8 May 1945, VE Day, a fact proudly recorded in their unusual wedding picture.**

Ken Eyre and his WAAF bride Mary Pilbin had to wait forty years before they saw their wartime wedding photographs.

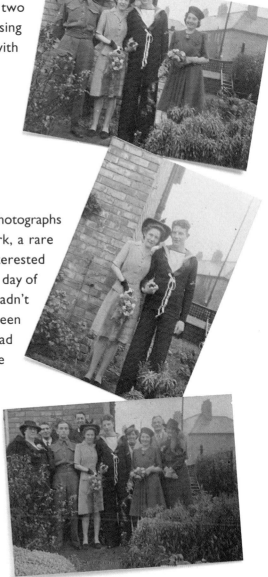

and his wife tried everywhere to get it developed but no one seemed able to deal with such an old film. They struck lucky in Sheffield – and forty years after the wedding Ken and his wife finally saw their wedding photographs.

Wedding rings sold in Britain were of a uniform utility nine-carat gold. One naval bridegroom-to-be nipped over the border to Letterkenny in the Irish Free State. There he chose a twenty-two-carat gold ring which he smuggled back for his bride.

Marriage brought into sharp focus the importance of looking alluring. Sometimes there was a feeling that before and after the wedding one or other would become disenchanted. Lily Gerrard, writing to her husband Charles, daydreamed in her letter about the end of the war:

Won't we be able to tell our grandchildren some tales when we sit in an armchair each side of the fire you with your bald head (you'll have to wear a skull cap) and pipe, me with my knitting, can you see us? If you were here now I should just kiss you and kiss you, you know like when you say, 'Eh! What's the matter with you?' do you remember? Oh, my dear, I do love you so.

Well, goodnight and God bless you, my love. I am your loving wife (I am so glad to be able to sign it so) Lily.

As an afterthought she added:

I say, don't go and grow bald, will you? I shan't know which way up you are when you come to bed.

In her parcels to Charles, Lily enclosed all sorts of useful presents, socks and cigarettes and so forth. She once sent a copy of *Lilliput* magazine, which she had never encountered before.

I didn't know what it was like till I got on the train. I started to glance through it then some man kept reading it over my shoulder (you know like they do on trains). I nearly had a fit when I turned to the nudes, I turned the pages quick. My face went hot and talk about blush, I was like a schoolgirl. I shan't read *Lilliput* on the train again. Still do you want it every month? I'll get it if you do. I am trying to save up to buy a chiffon nightie to thrill you when you come home. You know, one of those filmy flimsy things.

Honeymoon hotel bills were kept as reminders of the brief but happy days spent away from the realities of war. Some couples chose a resort hotel or a local guest house which could be reached easily at a time when all unnecessary travel was restricted. Others went for more luxury: in 1941 a night's stay for two at the Savoy Hotel in London, with dinner, cost just over £5.

Prothalamion – Gwyneth

Fleeter than swallow flickering on the warm wide west wind,
Flickering over the placid Trent from fields of hay,
Swifter than swallow flickering over corn soon ripening
My spirit wings out through the distance far away
To where a woman awaits me, burning out her girlhood.
A woman awaits me passionately, a bride, a bridal day.

A travelling and a waiting and a yearning and a looking to the city;
A fighting and a fasting, a resting and a shouting on the way;
And now a music calls me from the spaces, not of battle,
An aerial music calls me, but not from wings of grey
That gun-grapple in mid-air; rather a splendid singing;
A woman awaits me passionately, a bride, a bridal day.

Yearn not, weep not, cry not O My Darling, O Beloved:
The world will cease for us, and war be peace for us, I say.
When darkness folds the daylight, when purple closes whiteness,
We shall join the sound of singing and the Gods shall not betray
The days and hours of waiting and the high immortal longing,
O Woman waiting in passion, O Bride, O Bridal Day!

J.G. Meddemmen
10 August 1940

PREVIOUS PAGE: **One of Sir Archibald McIndoe's 'guinea pigs', Henry Standen, at his wedding to Ann, who nursed him at the famous East Grinstead hospital. He was severely burned when the plane he was navigating was shot down. He had managed to free himself, but realising the pilot was still trapped he ran back along the wing of the aircraft to help his comrade escape. Just then the aircraft blew up. McIndoe's revolutionary techniques as a surgeon saved the faces and hands of countless burned and maimed servicemen.**

Douglas and Christine Dunker had planned their wedding day to be 2 September 1939. As the day drew nearer it became apparent that war was going to be declared very soon. Some of the wedding guests rang to say they were unable to attend because transport everywhere was in chaos. The honeymoon in Folkestone was cancelled because the army had taken over the hotel; and at the Spread Eagle Hotel in Thame where they had planned a quiet dinner, staff refused to serve the newly-weds as they were rushed off their feet with soldiers everywhere. Douglas, a reserve in the Metropolitan Police, was called up the next day, 3 September, after Neville Chamberlain had declared, 'This country is at war with Germany.' For the next seven years Douglas and Christine scarcely saw each other – they reckoned their marriage really started in 1948. Nevertheless they celebrated their golden wedding anniversary in 1989.

Henry 'Mick' Stanley served in the Second World War in the RAF, 409 Squadron, the Pathfinder force, eventually completing at least sixty bombing raids for which he was awarded the Distinguished Flying Cross. Sixty raids was well above average, as life expectancy was limited in this high-risk unit. On 20 September 1943, the first anniversary of his wedding to Peggy, he wrote to her from RAF Gransden in Bedfordshire:

The wedding reception of John and Betty Charteris at Queen's Hotel gardens in Kandy, Sri Lanka, in 1945. John had written to Betty's parents asking their permission to marry their daughter, but the letter giving their blessing only arrived after the ceremony.

When I got back into the mess this evening I found your letter and your card waiting for me, for which I thank you very much and God Bless you for them, darling.

When I read them I had a strong desire to turn around and run right back home to you, but unfortunately it couldn't be done owing to this beastly war. Still one day – soon I hope – we will be able to settle down and lead a very happy life together. There never was a fellow happier, prouder, luckier and more grateful than I was on the day when God granted me the privilege of making you my wife and it's my one ambition to make you the best husband a girl could possibly have, for I love you far more than anything else on earth. The old song says that angels never leave heaven but I know that is not true because I happen to be married to one.

Goodnight, darling and God Bless and may I once again thank you for the happiest 365 days I have ever spent. The only time I shall be happier than I am now is when I tell you I love you on our golden wedding day. I love you, I love you, I love you, your loving husband,

xxxxx Mick xx

On 20 September 1992, Mick and Peggy did indeed celebrate their golden wedding anniversary.

The day after VE day, Sergeant Cope wrote a forces' airletter to Doreen, now his wife, waiting in Morden, Surrey:

9 May 1945.

My darling wife,

So at last it is really finished. People in England must have heaved an immense sigh of relief when Churchill announced the news. We did anyway.

VE Day we celebrated in a style all of our own. Our Div. led by 2RB crossed the Austrian border and now we are doing Army of Occupation several miles over the Austrian border.

The scenery over the pass, with the high snow-clad mountains, pure snow streams, chalets and hot sunshine, was beautiful.

The other end of the war scenes have been equally amazing. You have seen pictures of the beaten German Army of the last war straggling back to their homes with horse-drawn wagons. It was so like the pictures as to be almost unbelievable.

In the villages we were walking about intermingled with armed Jerries, no one taking the slightest notice of the other – the war was over.

A few days before we saw a great column of Jugoslavs – Chetniks moving along the road looking like King Charles' cavaliers. Hair down to

INDIAN POSTS AND TELEGRAPHS DEPARTMENT.

Received here at _____ H _____ M

O / NLT NIL 294/28 LONDON 18 IRC FIL RDTD AT BY
COLLECTED 27/31 NLT S /SGT R SCANLAN 942891
4 TH CORPS ORD FIELD PARK ABPOSIXTEEN

DEAREST BOB THE ANSWER IS YES ALL MY LOVE DARLING

From = STELLA BATES

Robert Scanlan received the
telegram from Stella Bates
accepting his offer of marriage.
The material for her wedding dress
was sent over from Burma, and she
noted that 'the cake was real', the
ingredients having been donated
by friends. She had known Bob
since she was a little girl.

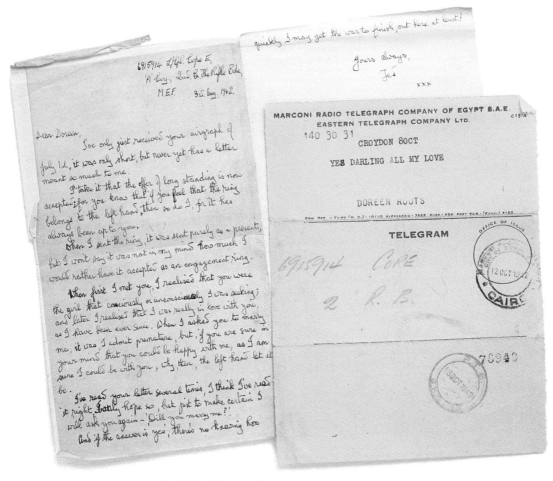

In the summer of 1942 Ted Cope sent a ring to his girlfriend, Doreen Roots. She took this as a sign that they were engaged and wrote enthusiastically to him at his base in the Middle East. Rather startled by this response he wrote back, asking her more formally if she would marry him. He received a telegram in reply: 'Yes Darling.'

their shoulders and in many cases curled like a girl's. But really they looked fine marching along with their wives and sometimes families on their wagons.

Then again the German Generals coming over the border to sign their surrender and afterwards lorryloads and columns of prisoners.

Soon I am sure they will reduce our service abroad to four years and then I should be home in July or August, but until all is definite we will hope for September.

I wouldn't have missed this historic scene for worlds, but I still long to be home again with you, my darling. I haven't had a letter from you for several days, but that is because our rapid movement has rather disorganised things, but soon there should be one.

So now with the war definitely finished I'll say cheerio, my dearest and long for our reunion soon.

All my love, my darling.

Ted xxxxx

Sylvia Wiley's story begins on VE day in Bedford: everyone was celebrating the end of the war in Europe.

My sister and I were Land Army girls stationed in Milton Ernest in Bedfordshire. We were sitting on the river bank just watching all the merriment, when two US airmen came by and stopped to talk. Our LA hostel was just four miles from their air base so our friendship blossomed and by the time they left for overseas we were talking seriously about a life together. Jerry, the one I was dating, was a twenty-year-old B17 pilot and from Texas.

He returned to England from France for a week's leave before returning to the States, this was March 1946. It was so brief and when we said our farewells at the railway station it was heartbreaking. We started to make plans for me to go to the States, papers were filled out and everything going well but taking time. As the days passed I began to have mixed feelings about leaving home and everyone I loved, not least of all my dog. I wrote to Jerry suggesting perhaps we could wait until he had finished university, so this is how it was to be. We continued to write but as time passed, as can happen, we started to lose touch and gradually our letters stopped altogether except for the odd card.

The years passed; Sylvia married and had two sons. Jerry's mother wrote to say that he too had married and had two daughters. In 1971 Sylvia was divorced from her husband and returned to her parents' home with her children. Out of the blue a letter arrived from Jerry saying he knew she was now single again and could he visit her?

After twenty-eight years apart, Sylvia was nervous that she might not recognise him; but when they met, rushing to meet each other in the middle of the road by the station, traffic going round them, she realised she needn't have worried. It was the same station where as twenty-one-year-olds they had said a tearful farewell. Jerry proposed to her, but Sylvia was looking after elderly parents and felt she shouldn't leave them. They promised to write and Jerry returned to the States. After her father's death, Sylvia's sister insisted she took a holiday and arranged for her to fly to Los Angeles. To her amazement Jerry was at the airport to meet her – all arranged by her sister. This time Jerry persuaded her to stay, and they married and lived for ten years in Texas. In 1984 they returned to England to live in the Cotswolds.

Decorations on a naval theme from the wedding cake of Iris Newling and Geoffrey Upham, a RNVR signals officer, who married in the spring of 1945. With dried fruit and other essential ingredients rationed in the Second World War, traditional wedding cakes were difficult to come by. Brides often had to settle for cardboard tiers, appropriately iced and decorated, concealing a much smaller fruit-cake beneath.

Anne Sullivan and Jim Roscoe on their wedding day, 7 July 1945.

Anne, a young woman in the ATS, and her soldier sweetheart, Jim Roscoe, a Desert Rat from Tobruk, mingled with excited crowds in London on VE Day, 8 May 1945.

The young couple were married two months later; they have never forgotten the thrill of that particular day:

Everyone had been given staggered leave to celebrate victory in Europe. Jim found his way to my camp and we decided that London was the place to be, right in the centre of the celebrations. We went to Piccadilly Circus and Buckingham Palace. How we got there I'll never know. I was giddy and heady with the most wonderful feeling. It was fireworks, thunder and lightning, electricity all at the same time. I can still see the devastation around us, whole streets razed to the ground, but we kept going until we reached the centre. For the soldier linking my arm this was the culmination of years abroad – Victory and a new life.

The crowds danced and sang right through to Buckingham Palace, thousands and thousands of merry people, linking arms and singing. The atmosphere was electric, everyone was so happy, all going along together, goodness knows where, we just went. I'll never forget that day: the wonderful feeling of exhilaration, youth, relief, longing, feelings of utter joy that life could begin in earnest. I was in love, with living, and that soldier linking my arm.

Yonder a maid and her wight
Come whispering by:
War's annals will cloud into night
Ere their story die.

Thomas Hardy
In Time of 'The Breaking of Nations'

ACKNOWLEDGEMENTS

Thanks to: Dame Vera Lynn DBE; Christabel Leighton-Porter; David Gainsborough Roberts; Corinne Gardner; Pat Lelliott; Mrs J F P Hambly; E W Cope MM; Helen Coleman; Mrs M W Ackroyd; Biddy Pledge; Tom Roberts; Mary Scott; R G Best; Joseph and Anne Rose Ryder; Cherry Richards; L Cowan; David Freeman; Len Wilson; John Barnes; Joe Oliver; D L Morrisson; Sergeant Dick Stokes RM; Mrs P Bettam; Edith Kup; David Barr; Christopher Portway; Mrs Rosemary Fellowes; Jim and Mary Wheeler; Sheila Squirs; Rose Campbell; Irene Homes; Freda Nightingale; Doris Ker; Linda Collin Page; Shirley Trustham; Doris Benjamin; C T Gerrard; Douglas and Claire Potter; Mary Sevenoaks; Frank Hall; John and Gwendoline Hampton; Margo Pearce Carey; Stella E Paine; Mrs I M Corry; Dorothy Smith; Mrs M Mosedale; Louis and Jessie Tibbert; Gerald and Mavis Bunyan; Reverend Canon W M and Mrs H Cook; T Kilfoyle; Helena Williams; Mrs M E Mace; Dr F G Hardman; Mrs K Cleasby-Thompson; Pamela Odell; Pat and Julia McSwiney; Peter W Merrill; Mrs M M Conquest; Freddy Bloom; Fred and Dorothy Lumley; Norman Boyle; Alf and Renée Sampson; Marion Makuch; Mrs D Browne; E L Byford; H Leslie Harrison; Bruce Pennell; R G Colman; Virginia Coan; Mary Taylor; John Dossett-Davies; Margaret McGrath; J G Meddemmen; Alan Merryweather; Jack and Marie-Louise Blackburn; T H A Potts; Nancy M Cohen; Elisabeth Reed; Frank Edwards; Pauline Richens; Reginald and Helena Blannin; Mrs P E Smith; Bryan Hunt; Stephanie Batstone; Tom and Doreen Bathurst; Mrs J Durk; Myra Forrest; Dr Gordon Charkin; F E Mace; Eileen Kisby; Ruby M Streatfield; Gwilym J Williams; Colonel D T W Gibson MBE; Mrs Elizabeth Dunkley; Mrs M W Taylor; Margaret Strong; L Price; Jim and Anne Roscoe; Stella Scanlan; Jean Hembry; Olive M New; Derek and Julie Read; Joan Brown; Mrs A R James; Mrs M Dickens; David Dickens; Fred and Marguerite Tustin; Douglas S Dunker; Jill South; Mr and Mrs H E Stanley; Sylvia and Jerry Wiley; Judith M Stockton; Val Wood; Jean Barr; E L Lancaster; John and Betty Charteris; Dame Barbara Cartland DBE; Fred and Vera Kelly; Brenda Hargreaves; Joe and Jean Fournier; Ken Eyre; Iris L Upham; Dorothy Hall; Lilian and Ramsay Bader; Dorothy Adkins; Mrs B M Hall; Joan MacFadden; Miss J Cooper; Mrs G Smith; W J Panckridge; Carolyn Marsden-Smith; Ciáran Headon; Greg Smith; Susan Proctor; Malcolm Brown.

Every effort has been made to trace all contributors. Any queries should be addressed in the first instance to the publishers.

Bibliography:

David Barr, *Twice Hooked,* Berkswell Books.

Judy Barrett Litoff and David C Smith, *Since You Went Away: World War II Letters from American Women on the Home Front,* Oxford University Press, 1991 (first publication of Lucille DesCoteau letter on pages 90-2 and republication of Anne Gudis letter on page 125).

Stephanie Batstone, *A Wren's Eye View,* private publication, 1976.

Freddy Bloom, *Dear Philip,* Bodley Head, 1980.

Helen and Bill Cook, *Khaki Parish,* Hodder & Stoughton, 1988.

Jeffrey L Ethell and Clarence Simonsen, *The History of Aircraft Nose Art,* Haynes Publishing Group, 1991.

Mark Gabor, *The Pin Up - A Modest History,* André Deutsch, 1972.

Juliet Gardiner, *Over Here,* Collins & Brown, 1992.

Tonie and Valmai Holt, *Till the Boys Come Home: The Picture Postcards of the First World War,* Macdonald & Jane's, 1977.

W J Panckridge, *Young Faces Young Lives,* private publication, Australia, 1991.

Christopher Portway, *Czechmate,* John Murray, 1987.

Victor Selwyn (ed.), *Poems of the Second World War: The Oasis Selection,* Dent, 1985 (first publication of Stephanie Batstone poem on page 143).

Annette Tapert, *Despatches from the Heart,* Hamish Hamilton, 1984 (first publication of Captain Alfred Bland letter on pages 66-7).

This England magazine, Cheltenham, Gloucestershire.

Wendy Webster, 'The Way We Won the War', *Independent on Sunday,* 15 December 1991.

Maureen Wells, *Entertaining Eric,* Imperial War Museum, 1988.

Woman's Own magazine, IPC.

Val Wood, *War Brides: They Followed Their Hearts to New Zealand,* Random Century New Zealand, 1991 (first publication of 'The Alphabet' by Ida Faulkner on pages 169-70).

Yank magazine, 26 September 1943 (first publication of Anne Gudis letter on page 125).

Additional picture sources:

Daily Mirror: page 19 *top*

Esquire magazine: page 20 *bottom*

Hulton-Deutsch Collection: pages 133,137

Imperial War Museum: pages 13, 23, 30 *left,* 32, 33 *bottom,* 37, 41, 50, 51, 52, 54, 66, 69, 71, 73, 74, 80, 91, 93, 99, 101, 102, 110, 111, 118, 132, 133, 137, 138, 139, 141, 150, 168, 170, 175

Knave magazine: page 36

Kobal Collection: pages 24 *left,* 28 *top,* 29 *right*

Press Association: page 17

Popperfoto: pages 148, 156

Royal Marines: page 21 *bottom*

Soldier magazine: page 20 *top*

Today/Mike Moore: page 64

Yank magazine: page 125

Photography by Andrea Heselton